In The Face of the Iguana, Patrick McKallick tells the dramatic stories of how fear-based beliefs, both cultish and religious affected his life, emotionally, physically and mentally and his eventual healing. This book is not just for all those abused by toxic belief systems, but also those recovering from addictions. The author relates touching stories of his painful abandonment by his troubled parents and his final internment in an orphanage. He tells dramatic and amusing anecdotes that preserved his sanity, and the utter desperation of his cunning and miraculous escape from a toxic, doomsday cult. We are taken on a journey of events as varied as hiding under the bed from his raging alcoholic father to descending into the depths of a 16th-century church's crypt where he gazed upon piles of human bones, the shock of which catapulted him unconsciously into a dark and ominous pit. We faithfully follow him as he describes the conclusion of the war in El Salvador and the mass fear and terror of the citizens of that country, to the comical circling of a vintage ocean liner in a beat up fishing boat with an old lady, a fisherman, and two young kids. This is not just a compilation of interesting stories, but clear guidance for anyone recovering from addictions including to fear-based belief systems and the ensuing guilt and anxiety. The author expertly provides revelations and insights into why we seek out toxic beliefs. Mr. McKallick reveals how his investigation of a surprising and astonishing field led to his incredible healing and liberation from the effects of PTSD. The author learnedly introduces evidential research that mitigated his anxiety due to abusive belief systems and the fear of death. He describes the ensuing collapse of this fear and the promise of an astonishingly beautiful after-life.

To Jay —
With very good
wishes!

Michael H.
"AKA Patrick"

THE FACE OF THE IGUANA

FREEDOM FROM TOXIC BELIEFS: A JOURNEY
IN HEALING AND TRANSFORMATION

Patrick J. McKallick

authorHOUSE®

AuthorHouse™
1663 Liberty Drive
Bloomington, IN 47403
www.authorhouse.com
Phone: 1 (800) 839-8640

Published by AuthorHouse 05/25/2018

ISBN: 978-1-5462-4070-9 (sc)
ISBN: 978-1-5462-4068-6 (hc)
ISBN: 978-1-5462-4069-3 (e)

Library of Congress Control Number: 2018905409

Print information available on the last page.

CONTENTS

ACKNOWLEDGMENTS

There are so many members of my family, friends, and acquaintances who played significant roles in the writing of this book. Many strangely inquired serendipitously as to the progress I was making assembling this book. Many times, I found myself being surprised at their insistence for completion. I followed their urging. It wasn't always easy to go back and relive the most painful days of my youthful experiences. I revisited painful memories cautiously, and when I finally considered the book written, there was a gentle push to go back and rewrite this part or that part I had omitted out of fear of treading into dangerous territory. I can now say that the job is finished, at least for now.

I want to thank all the members of my family, my grandparents, mother and step-mother for the significant roles of support and inspiration that you played in my life. Thanks to my sisters, Linda and Patty for your encouragement. Your help was substantial and meaningful to me since you experienced part of my ordeal which spilled over into genuine concern for my mental and emotional safety. Thanks for sticking by my side throughout this life together. Thanks also to Mike and Jan, for not only printing out a rough draft for editing purposes but your positive feedback on the contents, not to mention the beautiful T-Shirt you had made celebrating the birth of this work. I owe you both a profound sense of gratitude and admiration for what you do for others, and that includes the strangers that you meet along the road of life. To all my friends who took such a deep interest in this book's completion. I share my sense of accomplishment with all of you.

Thank you, Beverly, for mentoring me and for setting the example of how to flourish as a truly great author. Your books, so eloquently written, raised the bar for me to emulate such a high standard, however lacking I may have been in achieving such a status. My sincere gratitude also goes to Dr. Roxanne Henkin for recognizing my abilities as a writer and encouraging me to write on. Thank you for believing in me, and for your personal and professional generosity to help me grow as a budding writer. Mary Lou, without your tireless and professional editing of the manuscript, I would've spent endless more hours on the task and barely had accomplished what you so efficiently did in such a timely manner. I might add that your encouragement and positive feedback was a great motivator for me.

Thank you, Dr. Thomas, for your counsel on the inclusion of the Opposite Strengths program in the manuscript. Thank you also for reading the script on your vacation and the excellent review you afforded me. I would also like to thank you and your father, Dr. Jay Thomas for gifting the world with such profound wisdom and knowledge. This world would not be the same without it.

My most profound gratitude also goes out to Santa Fe Artist and evidential Medium Robert Carr. Thank you for the beautiful artwork you have produced for the cover of this book and for the encouragement and guidance that you afforded me in the realization of this project. I'm convinced that your work is divinely inspired and divinely manifested. Thank you for those gifts that you share with mankind.

Finally, I thank the TG, the TG's lieutenants, my father and all those other teachers that I was fortunate to have in this lifetime. I would like to acknowledge their assistance in helping me grow. You have helped me evolve into a more forgiving and compassionate human being. This lesson has been hard for me and continues to be, but I also recognize it's a work in progress. I thank all my helpers, seen and unseen. Without you, I wouldn't have had the courage nor the fortitude to have written this account of my journey through the valley of pain to the mountain heights of mental, emotional and spiritual redemption.

INTRODUCTION

"My story isn't sweet and harmonious like invented stories. It tastes of folly and bewilderment, of madness and dream, like the life of all people who no longer want to lie to themselves."
~ Hermann Hesse

"Do the difficult things while they are easy and do the great things while they are small. A journey of a thousand miles must begin with a single step."
~ Lao Tzu

As I review the significant events of my life, it's a wonder that you are holding in your hands this book which you intend to read. I should've died many times over, leaving you with the task of looking for another book that you might find interesting. The subject matter it covers is widely distributed across the boundaries of cultish institutions or churches. These are, for many, their drug of choice. And then, of course, are the cults that claim to be a church, but which are, in reality, factories of deranged cultish delusions. They specialize in inseminating the fertile minds of youth and those in search of truth, with vermin and filth. Churches can be a place of solace and reflection, or they can be shooting galleries, and I'm not talking about the kind you fire guns with. The addiction to beliefs is a big problem in the world. It becomes a drug like any other.

This is a story which really is made up of many stories. Some are interestingly entertaining, others dark and somber. Those pleasant and memorable experiences are what I like to call my life's oases in the desert. These sinister involvements which I relate to in this writing, I hopefully represent not as a victim, but as a learner in this cosmic classroom called Earth. It is said by many, that Earth is one of the most stringent learning laboratories in the Universe. I've read that we are courageous souls to have chosen this earthly experience. It can be a terrible classroom. But then, it's also a beautiful world, with beautiful people and picturesque lands and seas.

I initially started writing this book to help those, like myself, who have experienced the mental and emotional turbulence of Post-Traumatic Stress Syndrome. This experience was brought on by my addiction to the tyranny of toxic beliefs. But I share this story also for anyone who is struggling with the challenges of life. I write this account from the perspective of the learner and not the victim because I genuinely believe that we are here as learners. I guess my soul chose this experience because it was necessary to further my spiritual evolution. If you are confused or are wondering the meaning of these words, and if you are persistent in your reading, you will discover how meaningful these words are and how much sense it makes. Then again you may wish to dismiss that part, and that would be fine as well.

Reading this book may mean, for some readers, letting go and trusting their heart and not so much their intellect. That can be risky. At the same time, everyone must exercise their free will and trust only that information which feels right. If it doesn't feel right, don't believe it. One of my most profound learnings has been: Don't trust anything that anyone says, even those self-proclaimed authorities just because they said it. I do not by any means consider myself to be an authority, I am only a person who has had many experiences that might be shared in unison with so many humans who have been exposed to addictions, and in my case to the tyranny of aberrant belief systems. Accept only that which you wish, and discard the rest. There are no set rules to reading these pages and the subsequent thoughts that may follow.

I also started writing this book with a plan to share with my readers the many avenues of knowledge and healing that aided in my learning and recovery from religious addiction and the ensuing PTSD. These, in turn, assisted me, at last, to understand the nature of thought at its rawest core and the subsequent emotions that emanate from those thoughts. This knowledge finally helped me in my process to liberate myself from the toxic belief system that held me actively captive for 3 years of my life, and subconsciously for far too many more years thereafter.

I will share with you some of the most important milestones of knowledge and information that assisted me in my liberation. I intend to awaken your interest in the many evidenced-based practices that are available for you to explore. These proven practices may indeed help you in dealing with pesky belief systems that may have snared you. I share with you some of my most intimate moments of not only joy but of terror, events that I dared not relate to anyone before. Cathartic are these confessions emanating from the depths of my soul, transformational are the impacts on my existence. These narratives were not an easy task to write, but in retrospect, this labor became one that had a profound healing effect on me, mentally, physically and more importantly, spiritually.

I want to approach this subject not just from my perspective of the validity of my learning experiences, but also how these recollections served, literally, as life rafts to help me remember what *normal* life was like. These *life rafts* saved my life and I believe they were purposefully placed in my experiences to help me survive. More importantly, I speculate I experienced them so that I could continue to be of service to mankind, in one form or another. Perhaps these life events, are not terribly significant to the average person but are incredibly meaningful and relevant to me the experiencer.

The events of my life, as in the presence of mankind everywhere, demonstrate the resiliency of the human Spirit. The Merriam-Webster Dictionary defines resilience as: "1. The ability to become strong, healthy, or successful again after something bad happens; and 2. The ability of something to return to its original shape after it has been pulled, stretched, pressed, bent, etc." (Learnersdictionary.com).

If you are held in the clutches of any cult, a fear-based belief system, or any other addiction, or you are just experiencing bad times, it's my goal to give you some information and techniques to help yourself become free. These could include addictions to alcohol and drugs, food, relationships, sex, etc., and not just an attachment to toxic belief systems. When we talk about an addiction to a belief system, that may include political belief systems. These include the Church of Communism, the Church of Fidel Castro (and now Raul Castro), the Churches of the Republicans, the Democrats and the Libertarians, the Church of Kim Jong-un, the Churches of Putin, Trump, Lenin, and Mussolini. But this is also about the church of your local home-grown pulpit terrorist. He or she may include your local pastor or priest who preaches guilt, anger, fear, anxiety or terror through the deceitful veil of love, brotherhood, and so-called salvation.

These are the ones who, in the name of Jesus, Buddha, Krishna, or Mohammed or just every day God, make you feel angry, fearful, anxious, worthless, denigrated, depressed and or lonely, and do not by these provoked and imparted emotions, represent these spiritual masters or enlightened beings. They express the deranged leader's own ego and his or her desire for dominance over you and others within their grasp. I hope to share with you the basic principles of freedom from toxic beliefs and other addictions. These principles are the governing framework upon which you can possibly rebuild your life. By adhering to these principles, you will realize that you are no longer tied to the ideas and concepts conceived by others. You will declare your independence from the lies propagated by ignorant and fearful human beings. Of course, if your addiction is to substances, seeking professional help in a treatment center might be the first course of action you may want to take, at least, start your process of recovery through inquiry and then take action to become well again.

The purpose of this book is not to replace one belief system with another, and it is indeed not the replacement of one drug with another. It is, instead, an opportunity to provide as many options as possible that might assist you in your quest for freedom. More importantly, I hope that these stories of recovery may help you become not so much the participant but the observer without judgment or prejudice.

I invite you to consider all possibilities and adopt only those ideas which are safe for you. You have the right, and I might add, the obligation, to reject anything in this book or any other books, publications, broadcasts, etc., which you do not agree with or which goes against your principles or don't feel right for you.

I share with you my personal journey. Each one of us has our own quest to complete. Some segments of our missions may coincide and others may not. However, if there is any part of my journey that can assist you in achieving clarity of vision and understanding, then the trip was worth the effort. If there is at least one thought or principle that can help you to cut through the mire of this unpleasant trek, then it will have been worth it for me and hopefully for you as well.

The Universe, the Source, All That Is, the Divine Presence, The Unknowable, the Self-Organizing Intelligence of the Universe, however you want to call that Infinite, indescribable reality also known as *God*, has put many mile markers in my path to enlighten me and to wake me from the slumber of untruth. I want to share these with you as much as I possibly can. Many books, people, and inspirations have helped me along the way. I hope that some or all of them will help you or offer some comfort and help you on your path to recovery. I list these and will make reference to them as we go along. Although I may not cover all of them, each is worthy of review and familiarity. You will find a useful bibliography at the end of this publication.

The title of this book, *The Face of the Iguana*, is not designed to denigrate Iguanas nor to make monsters out of them. They are not exactly pretty creatures to gaze upon, but they indeed serve their purpose in nature. Actually, I am fascinated with Iguanas. As a child, I would observe Iguanas, especially when we would travel to the Pacific coast of Mexico in the summers. They would bask in the sunlight on rounded boulders or rocks. They would periodically blow their lower jaw pouches in and out to show their dominance, especially if their territory was threatened. So, you may ask why name my book after them. There are many reasons. First, iguanas represent the reptilian brain or the primitive brain. It is commonly known as the limbic or emotional brain which houses the amygdala which is responsible for the Fight/Flight/Freeze Response (FFFR). More on that later.

I also thought it appropriate to name the book after iguanas because they excel in the art of self-camouflage. They can be gentle and alluring, seemingly innocent and incapable of harm. Yet they can be very mean and vicious. Many an iguana owner has been attacked and bitten by the iguana's 120 razor sharp teeth. In many ways, the iguana not only represents the reptilian brain but also the deceptiveness of the illusions of danger and in this case the crafty cultists and the *artisans of disbelief* who ensnare the innocent and unsuspecting believers in their webs of terror and desperation. I was going to call the cult leader "the top iguana." However, in an effort not to denigrate the noble role that iguanas play in our eco-system, I decided that I would call the cult leader the "TG" or the Top Guano, and there is a story behind that one!

I hope you will enjoy your journey as we venture forth together in the land of lies, deceptions, trickery, mystery, laughter, and sadness.

Most identifying information in this book, such as names of persons and institutions, etc., have been changed to preserve the confidentiality of these individuals and/or organizations. However, the events in this book are described accurately as they occurred.

PART 1

STORIES WITHIN STORIES

CHAPTER 1

DEEP IN THE IGUANA'S DEN

"A teacher of fear cannot bring peace on Earth. We have been trying to do it that way for thousands of years. The person who turns inner violence around, the person who finds peace inside and lives it, is the one who teaches what true peace is."
~ B. Katie

"Many cults start off with high ideals that get corrupted by leaders or their board of advisors who become power-hungry and dominate and control members' lives. No group with high ideals starts off as a 'cult'; they become one when their errant ways are exposed."
~ Philip Zimbardo

We filed into the long, chandelier-filled hall. The TG (Top Guano=the cult leader) liked only the best. The TG worshipped money and possessions. But if you said that to the TG's face, you would have *blasphemed*. People walked somberly and took whatever seats they could. Some looked ghastly. Some had blank stares; others literally quivered with nervousness. One of the cult's highly placed lieutenants took the podium and barked instructions to the almost catatonic bodies present to begin the chanting. We chanted and chanted and chanted. It seemed endless. The stentorian humming of words was unintelligible and screeched of jibber-jabber. The drone of monotonous and hypnotizing voices overtook my consciousness, and I was in a trance, I noticed others were in that same deep, hypnotic stupor. This was a state that, at this point, was not unfamiliar to me. I could almost hear further instructions: *The punch vats have been set up for your convenience, so if you don't chant correctly, you will be directed to go have a cold refreshing drink.* I might as well have had a shot of that. In retrospect, it almost felt like Jonestown 1978 and the mass suicide directed by another deranged cult leader, Jim Jones.

My insides quivered nervously. The channeling meant that I would have to listen to that awful poison that spewed out of the TG's mouth. They were words of dread and lies that terrified our minds and hearts. I had been there eighteen months, not counting the two previous years as a long-distance participant. I was thoroughly brain-washed. I walked on eggshells in fear of being exposed to more horrible tales of doom and destruction and the kingdoms of the fictitious devils and demons that were everywhere, putting ideas in our heads and taking over our minds and bodies. If you think I exaggerate, think again. I thought, on many occasions: You didn't feel like this before, and you were very content. What has just changed? But I pushed the thought aside because the non-existent *forces of darkness* were putting those thoughts in my head. It was as if all my thinking faculties were ripped out of my willful control, except perhaps to eat and dress.

The mental anguish and terror, my own and that of others, were utterly beyond description. I can't adequately describe the abject anxiety and pain in which I found myself immersed. I was exhausted on every level of my being. As each day went by my terror increased. The chants we repeated were for protection or for divine intercession in some part of the world or other. They were uttered almost in desperation for some relief from the imaginary attackers of the would-be dark forces. But, according to the narrative of the cult, the powers of light would not protect us if we didn't ask.

God had suddenly become this puny little man, with a scraggly white beard that sat on this antiseptic, pine-smelling throne in some remote corner of the universe. He was made to look like he could easily be bullied by anyone or anything that even hinted at some form of aggression. God was nothing! He was a wimpy, worn-out, old man, conquered and enslaved by the non-existent devil and his lieutenants. It was easy to get the picture of what was going on in this madhouse of deceit, lies, and greed.

Toward the end of my eighteen-month immersion in the cult, it was no wonder the anxiety levels I experienced created terrifying dissociated states of consciousness. Ordinary things and experiences were no longer real. They were like blurred nightmares from which I could not, no matter how much I tried, wake up, or escape and flee for my life. These surreal experiences forced me into a state, not unlike any walking corpse - devoid of life, joy, and meaningful existence - could endure. I literally cut myself off from the reality of the world around me. This reaction, I later learned, my brain was automatically shutting down to protect me from going into shock. I now realize that was the face of the iguana, starring menacingly and directly into my eyes, seemingly murmuring, *I'm going to win, and you will be mine forever.* That was the face of the ugly iguana that represented the reptilian lurking in that part of my brain. The reptile that would haunt me and taunt me for a very long time afterward. It was post-traumatic stress disorder or PTSD.

It didn't take long for me to realize my mental and emotional health were in serious jeopardy. I had to do whatever it took to get away from this place, especially away from that monstrous creature I allowed to trick me, seduce me, betray me, and hypnotize me, robbing me of my personhood and my personal and financial resources. What stood out for me then, and now, is that almost every one of my cult-mates had numerous traumatic stories to tell about their lives. They appeared to long for healing. The traumatic events of my cult-mates became more and more evident to me as they related the bad things that happened to them, initiating either with their families of origin or from other events in their lives. Many had abandonment issues and/or mental, physical, emotional, sexual and generalized abuse issues. Some were suicidal.

One woman, in particular, a supposed friend of the TG, confessed that before arriving, she experienced several failed suicide attempts. She announced how the TG had reached out to her to join the church as a sign from the so-called divine ones, who beckoned her to change her life forever. Six weeks later, the woman looked worse than when she arrived. Her eyes bulged out with anxiety, and she openly condemned the TG as a monster and a predator of the weak and vulnerable. She pronounced the TG a scavenger, a person of deceit in pursuit of personal riches. She appeared to leave more suicidal than when she arrived. She filed a lawsuit, but we never learned the outcome. Many individuals did the same. I discovered later many of them won.

It wasn't until later in my professional experience and practice as an EEG Neurotherapist, cognitive behavioral counselor, and human development trainer that I recognized the pathology of cultist attraction. For me, the appeal to involve myself in this toxic belief system was the sincere desire to be healed from the abuses I experienced as a child, the abandonment issues, domestic violence, personal and familial attacks, and other issues that are too personal and painful to disclose in this writing. It was the terror promoted by a violent, alcoholic father, on one hand, and on the other, the deep longing for answers to the common questions of life, including: Why am I here? What's the purpose of my life? Why all the pain? Why the apparent injustices? Why do we have to suffer? Is there a heaven? Is there a hell?

The TG's psychopathology was also apparent. The paranoia, the schizophrenia, the delusions of grandeur and the deep-seated malicious narcissism became painfully evident. I later read the TG engaged in common and prohibited sexual practices with cult members. The TG was married with children and supposedly faithfully monogamous. The TG preached that oral sex was an automatic ticket to hell; no round-trip ticket on this one! Masturbation was out of the question, as was cunnilingus. Nevertheless, eyewitness reports were documented that the

TG engaged in all those practices. I suppose the TG was divinely exempt. How convenient! Participants who were LGBTQ were condemned just for being themselves. It's my understanding that many support groups formed after my departure to help the ex-cult members in their recovery from the PTSD that stemmed from their exposure to the vile and toxic environment of falsehoods and lies.

At times favorite memories of my youth surfaced to rescue me from the depths of depression and despair. Like riding with my grandmother and sisters in a beat-up old boat to an ocean liner, or endless hours we spent surfing the waves morning and afternoon on the beautiful, sun-drenched beaches of Acapulco during our summers of tropical content. There were memories of my high school, my friends, and the happy blossoming of my youth that became such an important mile marker in my life. I discuss these later as part of this roller-coaster journey.

CHAPTER 2

THE BEGINNING OF THE END

"When we totally align ourselves to belief systems based on the experiences of other people, I feel we lose something of our individuality in the process. The road to self-discovery and shaping a personal philosophy not designed by the doctrines of organizations takes effort, but the rewards are great."
~Dr. Michael Newton, Destiny of Souls

"We never see the great picture God paints for us because we are always standing on the canvas."
~ Robert Clancy, Author of Soul Cyphers.

My mental and emotional health were steadily declining. I knew escaping was necessary for survival, but I didn't know where to go or what to do when I got there wherever there was. Meanwhile, I did as much as I could to stay busy and work. Since I was a captive, and in the line of duty of service to the TG, I was ordered to do this and do that. We traveled to various cities, giving periodic conferences. I witnessed the lies and deceits of the grand deceiver as the TG gave speeches and channelings from the so-called high cosmic beings. It was all sugar-coated. Many times I thought, *You sick bastards, you are being led to the slaughterhouse. You don't have a clue what you are getting yourselves into.* I was there once myself. I remembered when I talked to other attendees and heard comments like, *The leader is indeed sent by God to heal me and the world.*

These were the TG's tactics. Recruit, recruit, and recruit more so a greater assortment of human and financial resources could be channeled into the organization. I overheard the TG's spouse confirm how much money the TG had made at a conference. It was followed by a list of items they could buy or trips they wanted to take. On another occasion, while standing nearby, I overheard the TG make some ridiculous fear-based statement. The TG's spouse angrily yelled out to the TG, *It's unbelievable how much you exaggerate!*

That woke me up. Suddenly, the god on the pedestal known as the great divine leader cracked and crumbled directly in front of me. The adored idol came crashing down. Imagine someone performing their bodily functions in full living color. Oh! That's right! The TG sits on the toilet and does what everyone does, and sprays with deodorizer like everyone else does when the toilet has been flushed. The TG burps and flatulates like everybody else! The deification of a human crashed with a resounding thump!

With a startled realization, I knew then, that I had been taken. I was hijacked by the bandits on the lonely road to nowhere. The iguana ate my lunch without my knowing. Snap! Gone! In a flash my job, my family, my hard-earned savings, and more importantly, my mental health and happiness disappeared without a single shot fired. The betrayal was stinging and hurtful beyond description. It sent me into a terrible depression.

After eighteen months of pure unmitigated hell, I found a possible way out. The organization was opening a branch south of their headquarters on the Pacific Northwest coast. I knew that if I could just get away from the TG and the lieutenants of the cult, I would stand a better chance of recovering my normality. By that, I mean, recovering from the numerous dissociative states and panic attacks I experienced. I felt so much fear my brain shut off the reality of the outside world to protect me from the imagined evil. That which I was fearing was the TG's paranoia and schizophrenia programmed in my conscious and subconscious mind. I was afraid of everything because the invented so-called forces of evil were everywhere and they were out to get me. Remember what I said earlier, God was a wimp? Plain and simple, He was a stupid little geek that all the imagined dark forces of the universe picked on! I was deceived into believing the existence of evil bullies in a perfect world that did not exist!

Being a cognitive behavioral counselor and EEG Neurotherapist and having studied and worked in clinical settings, I later recognized the TG's pathological mental illness. The TG had all of the symptoms of a functioning paranoid-schizophrenic with delusions of grandeur. The vile leader claimed to be queens and kings and superheroes of many a day gone by. The TG claimed to be a prophet! (I later changed that to profit!). I am not a Bible scholar. However, there is one passage that stands out above and beyond any that I have read and is the following:

"Beware of false prophets, who come to you in sheep's clothing, but inwardly they are ravenous wolves. [16] You will know them by their fruits. Do men gather grapes from thornbushes or figs from thistles? [17] Even so, every good tree bears good fruit, but a bad tree bears bad fruit. [18] A good tree cannot bear bad fruit, nor can a bad tree bear good fruit. [19] Every tree that does not bear good fruit is cut down and thrown into the fire. [20] Therefore by their fruits you will know them. (Mathew 7:15-20)

This passage alone summarized and confirmed what I needed to know and understand. It made all the sense in the world. It encapsulated my resolve to abandon the ship I was sailing on. And I did abandon ship!

The satellite branch was set up not too far from the headquarters up the Northwest coast in the Washington/Oregon area. I was one of fifteen cult-mates assigned to open and operate the new center. I got along well with my friends at the new place. I hung around the ones that seemed more normal. I settled in this old house that was tucked away in a secluded area deep in a pine forest. The TG was 200 miles away, and I breathed relief not having to deal with that offensive presence. I had the freedom to come and go as I pleased. There was no routine to speak of, and we were all encouraged, if not ordered to get a job and pay a monthly room and board plus a fifteen percent tithe to fund, as I discovered, the TG's extravagances.

I found a job at a well-known department store in a nearby town close by. Finally, I was out in the sane world, so to speak. I had my first taste of freedom! It felt so good! One day, I was restocking linens and draperies in the store's stock room. I had a moment of awareness like someone waving their hands in front of my face saying, *Hey I want you to pay attention to this!* That was the beginning of many of what I called my quiet moments of complete awareness.

Moments like these became more frequent in my life. I learned to be still, even in the middle of my busyness. I learned later in life that these moments were sacred and are what I refer to the "Still Small Voice" that speaks in whispers across the emptiness of time and space. I capitalize those words because my Inner Wisdom tells me that they come from a Higher Source, my Higher Self. I also learned to recognize these events when they happened and to respect them and to learn from them. I learned to be receptive to them.

I was keenly aware of my coworkers around me laughing and joking and really enjoying themselves and I thought to myself, why are these people so happy and I am so afraid and anxious? And, like a dark hood ripped off my head, I heard the Still Small Voice say, *they don't believe what you believe and think what you think. Your thoughts are making you fearful.* It hit me hard. Oh, my God, I let myself be brainwashed and programmed to believe in lies. One would think that obvious, but unless a person has been immersed in a sea of lies and deceptions, one loses the correct compass heading that points to the truth. Cults are designed to confuse and scramble the mind to internalize a particular software, which is written with one purpose and one purpose only; to control the members to obey the dark whims and desires of the cult leader. The brain is seized and locked, and the cultists have the keys, or so they would have you believe.

Instantly, I realized the power of my thoughts! These anxious feelings came from these terrifying thoughts! Without the ideas, I would not have anxious feelings. Without the stories, I would not be fearful and anxious. At that time, I realized the power of thought and how it had changed my life! I became agitated and angry. I cursed the cult leader and the arrogant and condescending lieutenants that made my life miserable. It was unbelievable how I gave my power, my money, and my energy away to people who had only one thing in mind: power and control over me and all who were trapped by them. As I write this, I remember a quote from Carlos Castañeda: "We either make ourselves miserable, or we make ourselves strong. The amount of work is the same." I was making myself despondent and not healthy. This happened because of the thoughts I entertained.

CHAPTER 3

THE PLIGHT AT THE END
OF THE TUNNEL

"Everything that happens to you in life, good and bad, provides lessons from which you can learn and grow spiritually. Always look for that lesson, and shine within the silver linings you discover along the way."
~ Robert Clancy (Author of Soul Cyphers)

I thought long and hard about my next step. I contemplated the pluses and minuses, and they all added up to freedom. But the freedom that was inevitably going to be hard earned. With some trepidation, I gathered enough courage to take my next step, but it wasn't without doubts and fears. So, one lovely day in late May, I decided to make my next move to freedom.

I knew an acquaintance and a fellow cult-mate named Jeff. He managed to rent a room from a family named Taylor who were quasi-active members of the cult/church. The Taylors lived inland from the coast, and very close to the department store where I was working. Fortunately, I had developed a cordial relationship with them over the past year. One day, I went over to their house under the pretense of visiting Jeff.

I knocked on their door not knowing what kind of reception I would receive.

"Oh! Hello Patrick! Come in! It's great to see you again!" said Mrs. Taylor.

I sighed relief at her warm welcome. I didn't know exactly what effect my unannounced visit would have. Her husband, fortunately, was not at home at the time. I sighed relief as I didn't want any unnecessary opposition.

"What brings you to these parts of the forest?" she literally and pleasantly inquired.

"Well, I work not too far from here, and I thought I would come to say hi to you and to also chat with Jeff if he's in."

"Jeff isn't here, but he generally gets home in about a half-hour."

We exchanged small talk for about 10 minutes. Mrs. Taylor graciously offered me a cold drink, and we sipped our refreshing beverages and talked about this and that. It was just idle chat, at times tedious and mostly inconsequential at best. Mrs. Taylor loved to chit-chat, and it was mainly about trivial matters concerning her role as housekeeper, being a mother to an autistic child, and dealing with a seemingly absent-minded husband who was a professor at a local community college. He apparently was oblivious to everything she held near and dear to her, and that unnerved her beyond imagination. Without warning, I suddenly became her therapist who listened patiently and thoughtfully.

My deceptive listening manner, though, betrayed her confidences. My mind was elsewhere. Securing passage on the ship to freedom which their house had become for me, was my top concern. I was busy plotting and pretending to be listening. My face lied. I nodded intermittently giving the air of compliance with her need to be heard and alleviate her frustrations. I was merely polite with an ulterior motive. It was not the noblest of human interactions.

Mrs. Taylor also had a curious obsession with people's body language while they made either a positive or negative statement. She couldn't fathom why people would negatively shake their head, back and forth, from left to right while they made a positive account, and the reverse, down and up while they made a negative comment. She lectured me about this curious habit of mine that I was oblivious to doing.

"You know Patrick you have made 3 positive statements while negatively shaking your head! That's totally incongruent!!" In an instant, it seems the roles were reversed. She became the counselor, diligently lecturing me on the significance of being congruent with the polarity of our statements. I never forgot her *mini-lectures* on the extreme importance of maintaining verbal and body language congruency at all times. From that day forward, I was conspicuously aware of keeping my body language in the agreement with whatever comment I was making.

I kept her busy talking about trivial matters such as her body language congruency fixation. She had other pet peeves, and I fed these my seeming continued interest to steer her clear of any topic having to do with the cult or the TG. During a noticeable pause in our conversation, I seized the pregnant pause in her tirades to interject the feigned reason for my visit.

With apparent awkwardness, the words blurted out: "Mrs. Taylor there is one problem I am having, and I wonder if you might be able to help me." She was caught off guard. Her carefully assembled list of favorite topics suddenly collapsed, apparently, much to her chagrin. She looked at me quizzically with a slight hint of concern.

"Of course, Patrick! What is it?"

"You know that the mother house has set up the branch on the coast," I said very shyly.

"Yes, of course, you are living there, and Jeff was living there before."

"Well you may not have known, but I have been commuting back and forth to work here, and quite frankly, whatever little I make is being spent on gasoline," I lied.

I told her flat out that I couldn't afford the commute to the house on the coast. So, I came right out and asked her if I could rent a room from them.

"Sure Patrick, I have no objections, but the only condition would be if you could share space with Jeff and of course you would have to discuss that with him. He should be home shortly."

I felt a surge of hope. It felt like the prison warden had given me a sudden promissory reprieve. "Sure, I know that would be necessary, and that's one of the other reasons why I'm here." I meekly responded smiling broadly inside. Jeff had procured many odd jobs, a few of them painting houses.

I heard a car pull up in front of the house and a car door slam.

"That must be Jeff!" Mrs. Taylor cheerfully said. Anne Taylor seemed to be a woman of eternal optimism. I wondered how that could be, and still belong to a cult steeped in terror. That was bewildering to me. But I suspect she hadn't yet bitten into the poisoned apple like the rest of us.

Jeff's paint-splattered jeans were the first to appear through the squeaky screen door. Anne Taylor was a fan of fresh air, even if the temperature outside was far below my comfort level, her house had to be thoroughly ventilated. The children were often sick. I wonder why!

He entered the modest house without having seen me, but surely, he had seen the white Dodge station wagon. Or perhaps he didn't, he tended to be aloof and distractible, severely affecting his observational skills if he had any.

Jeff came into the living room. His gaze fell on me triggering surprise that seemed to instantly morph into suspicion. I sat comfortably in the high wingback leather chair in Mrs. Taylor's comfortable living room. My heart began to pound. Here was the person who had the ultimate key to my immediate freedom. He stammered. "Patrick, what brings you here?"

"Just visiting Mrs. Taylor," I managed to meekly utter. He shook his head affirmatively, his suspicion never disappearing from his bronzed brow. He did not look very pleased. I was uncertain if he suspected why

I was there, but at this point, I didn't care. I had to get away from those people at the other house at all costs.

"Get something to drink Jeff and come have a seat with us." Mrs. Taylor said casually. "I made a fresh batch of lemonade."

"Sure, I am pretty thirsty. It's been a hot grueling day." Jeff vanished through the swinging doors of the dining room into the kitchen. He quickly returned with a glass of lemonade filled with noisy ice cubes. They seemed to announce his displeasure with my sudden and unexpected visit. I sensed resentment for the ostensible incursion on his sacred territory.

We spent about 10 minutes in idle talk. Jeff talked about his house painting and the work that was involved and if it was worth all the work for seemingly so little money, etc. I thought to myself that was one job I did not want. He abruptly turned to me and asked how things were back at the coast house.

"Well, that's precisely what Patrick and I wanted to talk to you about." Mrs. Taylor spontaneously interjected. I was grateful for her timely rescue of the awkward direction the conversation was heading.

His brows raised suddenly, seemingly confirming his suspicions as he peered intensely at me. Jeff was a very passive individual. He had a reputation for being a softy and a yes person, in short, he was a people pleaser. I knew that, and I confess that I had deliberately targeted that weakness of his character to get my way and move out entirely from the satellite branch.

"Patrick is having difficulties keeping up with his financial obligations at the coast house, especially given the fact that he has to commute 40 miles to come to work and return home again."

Without giving him a chance to respond, I spoke up quickly: "Jeff, you know how difficult it is to pay the dues at the other house. You know how much they demand from us regarding money and volunteering of our time for chores and all the other work that is expected of us. I'm just asking for some space where I can bring my sleeping bag, and promptly leave to go to work. I promise to stay out of your way, I promise!" I pleaded pitifully.

Thankfully, Anne, once again, quickly intervened on my behalf. "Jeff, I have told Patrick that I don't mind him staying here, but he must stay with you in the basement if that's OK with you." "I understand Mrs. Taylor." Without hesitation, he said: "Let's go talk downstairs and see how we can make this work." "Sure!" I instantly agreed, and we promptly scurried down the stairway into the converted basement.

Dropping abruptly on his bed, he uncharacteristically growled: "You know Patrick, I understand the problem you are facing, but you could've come directly to me without having to go through Mrs. Taylor first," he intimated passive aggressively at the confirmation of this apparent intrusion.

"Jeffrey, I intended to do just that, but since you weren't here, I had to tell Mrs. Taylor why I came by and the nature of my dilemma. I am really in a bind." I pleaded almost tearfully. "I know your space is important to you and I will do everything I can to not violate it. It's just that I make so little money at the store and a lot of it is going to pay for gas." I again lied.

"I understand that Patrick but I also need my own space and some privacy to be with Becky."

I knew he was courting a fellow cult member and he wanted to be alone with her without the other members of the cult snooping about their business. She was my friend as well, and I was aware of the pretentious romance. Becky didn't seem very smitten with soft-spoken Jeff. Of course, I understood their need for "private time," and it wasn't for sex, as that was strictly prohibited, or so I was led to believe.

"Listen," I said in an imploring tone, "You just let me know when you need to be alone and I will make myself scarce." And without giving him a chance to speak, I abruptly and regretfully said without thinking, "I will pay you extra money a week if you want me too." My desperation was really showing at this point.

He remained quiet and pensive, as he looked at the bare floor. He occasionally glanced over at me. His countenance softened, as I accurately predicted it eventually would. I sighed quietly inside. But then he dropped the bomb that I wasn't prepared for.

"No, you need the money for gas, instead of paying me extra money a month you can help me out with the painting of some my houses. I'll pay you half the minimum wage." That was about $1.05 an hour if I recall correctly.

I quickly agreed. I knew Jeff was taking advantage of me. But I knew that I would be gone very soon, and if he got one house out of me, he could consider himself very lucky. And furthermore, if the cult didn't give me permission, I was skipping town anyway and they would just have to come after me like they had with so many others. But in my case, they would have to hunt me down in Mexico. So, I made arrangements to move into the Taylor's the next day.

In retrospect, I think I failed miserably at trying to hide my desperation. I suspect Jeff picked up on that and was more understanding. I dared not tell him that I couldn't be around those people and that place anymore. I feared being accused of treason. Many things he said and did, gave me hints that he too was on to them and was becoming increasingly disillusioned. He told me many times that he didn't want to talk "shop" meaning anything to do with the cult or the church. I told him I didn't either. So, the matter was settled.

I informed Mr. Albert, the elderly director of the house about my new arrangements. He was a kind and understanding man who was soft spoken and learned. He was a student of the old metaphysical schools or mystery schools as they were so strangely called. I often wondered how an intelligent, reasonable, and kind man could also be deceived into submitting to the TG and the cult. It just confirmed in my mind the hypnotizing power of belief systems. I suspected he was vulnerable and a very lonely man and this gave him a reason to exist. He welcomed conversations and visits from the members of the branch. In many respects, I was grateful that he was put in charge of the house. Mr. Albert agreed to let me go, provided of course that I keep up with my dues and other obligations. He said he could open my bed up to another member who wanted to transfer to the house.

With a broad smile on my face, I thanked him profusely, I was ecstatic to learn that I could break entirely away from the branch house at the coast. I immediately set out to gather some but not all of my belongings. I returned there occasionally to pay my dues and attend to my assigned chores like distributing and posting church conference announcements on bulletin boards of colleges, student centers, health food stores and metaphysical bookstores. However, I made my stays at the coast house very short with the excuse that I had to get back to work.

I stayed at Anne Taylor's house for about 4 months. Jeff did manage to corral me into helping him with an old frame house he was about to paint. The house belonged to a sweet elderly woman. She offered us cold drinks and snacks. Frankly, it was the only benefit I got out of the deal. I paid dearly for my short stay with Jeff. He put me to work scraping old paint from the frame house siding. It was grueling hard work, and the more I scrubbed paint, the angrier I got. It indeed was not worth half the minimum wage he so generously paid me. We did finish the house, and I swore I would never pick up another steel brush or repaint another house in my life. Jeff was eager to take on more house painting jobs, but I was in the middle of my plan to escape to safety. I was on my way out. So, I kept putting him off telling him that I had a serious family matter to resolve. He was none too pleased, but accepted it, much to my relief.

Going to the coast house was not always pleasant or without risk. On one occasion I went to pay my house dues, I unexpectedly heard the TG in one of the rooms adjacent to where I was conducting my business. I was unaware the TG was going to visit the house. My heart seemed to have jumped out of my chest with the frantic beat of a thousand drums. I dropped what I was doing, and I told whoever I was talking with, I was late for work and had to leave. Otherwise, I would be fired. I was noticeably disturbed, and this worried me. Any sign of wanting to abandon the cult was high treason, punishable by the equivalency of death. I ran out of the house and jumped in my trusty Dodge station wagon and drove off like a mad person. The incident made my resolution to escape more urgent and desperate. I never wanted to look at or hear the sinister voice of the TG ever again. And I never did.

CHAPTER 4

ESCAPE OR THE CLOWN?

"Spirit is outside of time and space. The Spirit in you is the eternal, timeless part of you that is One with the God that created you. It is the divine consciousness that is the foundation of your expression in space and time."
~ *Pamela Kribbe*

It's a wonder to me how people can live in a climate that is mostly damp, cloudy, foggy, and dull for the majority of the time. And they carry on with their lives as if the cold droplets of moisture dripping from their eyelashes was just standard! On top of that when you ask them if they liked living there, they cheerfully told you they wouldn't live anywhere else. I didn't understand it then, and I certainly don't understand it now. It's not just the Pacific Northwest, but generally all up and down the Western coast of the United States, with a few exceptions of course.

Having grown up in a semi-tropical to tropical climate most all of my life where most of the time it was sunny and cheerful, I found living there to be most depressing. Being in that part of the U.S. saddened me even without all the drama of the circus I was attending called a "church." And if it wasn't a church, then it definitely had to be a cult. The organization had all the comedic complications of a circus, and the very dark nuances of the clown turned murderer. So, if it was to be assigned a genus or a species name would it be: "Cultus Sinistrus"? Or would it be "Circus Terribilis"? How about we settle for both because that's exactly how to describe this hellish outfit that I was determined to escape. It was a cultish circus that was terrible and sinister.

The dull, cloudy northwest coast weather contributed to the severity of my depression. I suffered from SAD or Seasonal Affective Disorder. It's a wonder I could go to work. There were intermittent breaks in the weather. There were sunny days, which I loved. But for the majority of the time, it was mostly cloudy, foggy or both. The weather vacillated as did my moods. The tall, beautiful pine trees of the forests in the Pacific Northwest were a treasure of nature's gift of healing. I would take long walks and sit under the pine trees and gather my thoughts and feelings. Sometimes, I relaxed, sometimes I cried. I missed my family, and I wanted to see my grandmother before it was too late. That kept me going, as did the thought that I would one day walk away from this nightmare to freedom.

I was tired. I was weary and disheartened. I desperately sought an escape route, the sooner, the better. It seemed like the only option. I racked my brains to come up with a solution to this grim situation. One morning, I awoke from a profound sleep, and like a flash of lightning, I came up with this incredible plan. I don't know where it came from, but I thought it was brilliant. My intuition told me it would work to free me.

The plan was to announce that my grandmother's health was failing and she had decided to divide up her estate before she passed away. Of course, in my mind, the "estate" was in the Millions of Dollars. Let's go for broke! If I told the local director of the branch house of this inheritance, surely it would travel quickly up the ranks to the TG. I would say to Mr. Albert that I needed to be there right away so I could receive hundreds of thousands of Dollars which I would bring back to the organization. I figured my brilliant plan would play right into the hands of the avaricious TG who would not hesitate one bit to grant me permission, provided, of course, I returned with the money. And that wasn't going to happen!

I imagined them planning to leave as soon as possible on trips to Europe or South America, on buying new clothes, jewelry, or anything else they wanted. And I just smiled and thought to myself, *I got you just like you thought you had me.* I knew their game, and I had to play into it. But I had to be very careful. Others had tried to make up stories about their families. Some claimed they had to leave because of deaths in the family or this reason or another. When they didn't return, they caught up with them, and the TG filed lawsuits against them for breach of contract. (We had to sign contracts to support the organization or face legal action should we default). That stopped after about 5 or 6 years because the church was countersued for fraud and damages of all types including mental and emotional anguish.

I was glad to hear the church lost most of the cases. The payouts were in the millions. They quickly rethought their strategy. Those whom they could change their mind and convince to return, where immersed into submission with dogma and reprogramming. It was like Mao's Chinese "re-education camps." The horror stories were many. Many lost their minds and became walking zombies. Some committed suicide. Some escaped again and filed lawsuits. But the TG escaped harm, claiming the lieutenants acted without consent. The TG actually sacrificed the most loyal followers for self-serving benefits. I was determined that this was not going to happen to me.

So, shortly after I had my dream, I was due to go pay my "dues" to the coast house. I nervously called Mr. Albert and asked him if he would be available so I could talk to him. He always seemed to welcome any opportunity to chat.

"Sure Patrick, when do you want to come down?"

"As soon possible Mr. Albert because I have something vital to tell you and then I have to scoot back to work."

"I was going to run some errands," interrupted Mr. Albert, "but I'll make sure to make time for you." We agreed on a time, and I thanked Mr. Albert. I hopped in my car with the usual dread of having to go back to the coast, but this was for the real deal, my final escape. My mood improved significantly.

"Mr. Albert! Thank you so much for waiting for me!" I said as I caught my breath running to his office. "I was so worried I wouldn't find you and what I have to tell you is so critically important." "No problem Patrick. Tell me what's going on, you seem to be preoccupied with something."

"Well, in a way I'm apprehensive about my grandmother. I received a call from my father in Mexico this morning, and he told me that she was not doing well and her health was failing." "I'm terribly sorry to hear that Patrick!" said Mr. Albert, who seemed genuinely concerned. "Does this mean you have to leave to go there? I don't know if headquarters will give you permission," he added somberly.

"Well, there's another part of this that should be of great interest to the Church and the TG (I named the cult leader), and it concerns an early disbursement of her estate which is in the millions of Dollars. My father said that I needed to be there for the distribution. Otherwise, I would not get my share. My grandmother insisted on it." I blatantly fibbed. His eyes seemed to bug out of their sockets. Money! That caught his attention.

"Oh, that's quite a different story, isn't it?" he said very animatedly, as the wattle of his turkey neck flapped excitedly. I was suddenly very disillusioned with this noble old man who seemed so wise and kind. Was he hoping for a cut? The most he would get would be a pat on the back from the TG. I thought to myself, "You're a foolish old man! There was not going to be any money, and you're not going to see my ass again." They would have to go to Mexico, and they won't have a clue where to find me.

"Oh, don't worry Patrick, I'll get on it right away, or "tout de suite" as they say in France!" he giggled to himself. "Thanks a million, Mr. Albert, and please let me know right away so I can make my travel arrangements." "Oh, indeed Patrick, I'll get on it right away!"

I ran back to my car as if I was in a terrible rush mainly because I wanted to avoid talking to anybody in the house. One cult mate tried to stop me. "Sorry man! I'm late for work. Later!" and I peeled off as fast as my trusty little Dodge could drive me away. God, I loved that old beat up car! It was so faithful to me. It never broke down. It seemed like the two of us were plotting our escape together.

I felt sorry for Mr. Albert, as he was a kind, old man in spite of his apparent flaws. As if I was flawless! I knew he had been duped just like the rest of us. I also knew that his loneliness was a big problem for him. He sought the company of kindred souls, but I just wasn't going to be the same to him anymore. Sorry Mr. Albert, but I have a life to live, I thought as I drove away, laughing at the shaking image of his gelatinous turkey neck wattle.

THE CULT CLOWN

Every school has a clown, and every classroom also has a clown. So, we know about the school or class clowns. These are the kind of people who are continually needing to entertain everybody around them, regardless how dark or dire things seem to be. If you haven't heard of cult clowns, you will now. Kerry was our cult clown. He was also like the typical party guest who, at some point gets sick in the punch bowl. He said things impulsively that many times got him in trouble. But his need to cut up was seemingly compulsive and to the point of being repulsive. He joked about anything trivial. As time went on, I noticed that his clowning around showed up more like fear or nervous laughter. He avoided talking less cult shop or dogma ramblings than he had before. Thankfully there were fewer news flashes from the so-called cosmic beings. And the reason was apparent, it was filled with fear, damnation, and horrible news for us and all of mankind. It was the nasty world we seemed to be living in, the cataclysms that will befall us and the dire peril of our souls if we messed up, and on and on it went.

At this point in my cult career, I was sick and tired of hearing that crap. I cringed when anybody said anything dark with a sinister twist. I made a habit of walking away from conversations, or I'd distract myself, so I didn't have to listen to the BS. That was the main reason why I moved to the other house, to be free from all that. It was also, at that time, that I began to read a very positive book that, allegedly had been transmitted through some mystic decades earlier, and oddly enough, by the same "cosmic beings" that the TG was purportedly channeling. Channeling, in this case, meant the TG's putrid sub-conscious mind vomiting the stench of her psychopathology, i.e., schizophrenia, paranoia, etc.

The messages in the book I was reading were entirely upbeat and emphasized positive thinking, etc. This was a big moment of discovery for me. I thought to myself, how could these make-believe cosmic beings who were so optimistic before, suddenly turn around and be such contrary entities decades later? The messages from both sources were as opposite as to what the darkness of night is to the light of day. That was my first clue that the TG was a fraud. The TG rode on the coattails of others' success from the past to boost the ego and make millions in the process. Furthermore, it is evident to me and many others that plagiarism ran rampant among the publications that came out of the organization.

Back to our cult clown Kerry. I had the book in my possession. Let's call the book "The Revelations of the Cosmos," not its actual title, but let's pretend that's what it was for the sake of this writing. Well, to have the Revelations book on one's person was tantamount to high treason. We were strictly forbidden to read or to even have the book in our property. I think the reasons were pretty obvious. The comparisons of both texts were so obviously contradictory that questioning by the followers would probably be too much to handle and the whole organization could possibly collapse. I used the book to begin my deprogramming to make my exit as smooth as possible and to alleviate the anxiety and depression I was going through. I am convinced that had I not had that book, I would not be writing these words today. The help was heavenly sent, I am convinced of that to this very day.

On one occasion, I was at the coast house paying my "fees" and gathering some belongings to take to Anne Taylor's home. For the past 4 months living at the Taylor's, I had slowly packed grocery bags full of clothes and odds and ends. To avoid suspicion, I hid the things in my laundry bag and carried them out to my car. If anybody asked, I had lots of dirty clothes to wash. I found neat hiding places in their basement to store my odds and ends. I didn't think either Jeff or the Taylors would betray me. But I couldn't take that risk.

On this particular day that I was at the coast house, our beloved cult clown Kerry was sweeping the room or doing some cleaning. I previously had shared this room with him along with two other cult-mates. I minded my own business tuning out Kerry's endless diatribes and silly jokes and giggles. Suddenly and without a hint of warning, he uncharacteristically said something like: "The TG in this week's channeling said that if we didn't chant more, a tsunami was going hit the Pacific Northwest." I was suddenly outraged and without thinking said: "Hey listen, Kerry, I have no interest in hearing all that negative crap if it's going to happen so be it!" He stared at me in disbelief. His mouth hung open like a deranged cat with its mouth wide open with a dead mouse stuffed neatly in it. He looked at me like I just called the Pope an asshole. Then I made the biggest mistakes of all. In a full-blown rage, I said: "Furthermore, in the Revelations book, so and so cosmic being said that what we put our attention on our energies flow into and we take on the vibratory patterns of that upon which we pay our attention."

As soon as the words left my lips, he, in turn, slammed his broom on the floor. He angrily yelled: "So you are reading that book? You know you're not supposed to." I retorted: "So, I think we have a little contradiction here, don't we?" The TG says one thing, and the Revelation Book says the opposite, and supposedly it's all coming from the same source! Isn't that interesting! Somebody is obviously telling some big fat lies, don't you think?"

I knew I had made a mistake and if anyone would turn me in it was going to be a loose cannon, Kerry. "'I think I'll need to turn you in for violating the rules." He yelled. "Go right ahead asshole! See if I give a fucking shit!"

Cursing was a big no-no. It meant (and today I laugh my head off at this stupidity) that you were possessed by "cursing entities!" Well, I must've been full of them because I didn't ever recall relishing my expletives so much like I did on that day!

What impressed me the most about this little dialogue with Kerry, the cult clown was how he became so enraged when his belief system was challenged with hardcore evidence. He seemed to panic at the thought that he too had been taken for a ride. It looked like his whole world was crumbling right under his feet. He turned into a raging monster. I ponder today, isn't that why people, in general, get so defensive when their belief systems are confronted with evidence they had not previously considered. It can get very nasty, indeed.

He came after me and raised his fist to my face, but held back as he was about to follow through with the punch. "Go ahead Kerry hit me," I angrily confronted him. That would be cause for worse punishment, and he knew it.

"I'm turning you in, Mr. Albert won't like this at all."

"Go ahead, Kerry! I'll tell him that you got verbally and physically violent with me, that you threatened me with physical violence. That'll make us even, won't it?"

I picked up my bags of meager belongings and walked quickly out of the house, cussing as I left. My efforts to abandon the place were reinforced with renewed determination. I jumped into my car and drove away with a delicious sense of satisfaction I had put the idiot Kerry in his place. I smiled smugly. I got the son-of-a-bitch, and it felt like I was getting the TG, as well. I laughed as I drove back to the Taylor's. But, I also started to worry what the loose cannon would do.

A week went by, and I had not heard from Mr. Albert yet! All kinds of scenarios were crossing my mind, from Kerry telling on me, to one of the Lieutenants of the cult coming down to take me back to headquarters for processing, which meant something like a trial. The great viper (the TG) presided at these tribunals, and I could not face being in that presence anymore. I thought to myself that if that happened, I would consider suicide rather than to have to face that beast.

A week later, I heard that one of the top lieutenants was at the coast house. Mr. Albert called Anne Taylor's home and spoke to Jeff. He told him that he and I had to report to the coast house for a meeting with the Lieutenant. I froze with fear. I thought that the best course of action, in this case, was to take the offensive. So, I called Mr. Albert immediately after Jeff had given me the message.

"Mr. Albert, I can't make it to the meeting because I'm waiting for a call back from Mexico as my father wanted to urgently speak with me about my trip down there. Apparently, there is some important information he wanted to pass on to me. At least that's what Mrs. Taylor told me. Have you spoken to anyone about my trip?"

"Oh Patrick, I'm really sorry, but I have been swamped, and whenever I've called up there, Brian or Peter aren't available. But Brian is here now, and we can discuss it with him. He also wanted to talk to you about an incident that you had with one of your roommates." I turned beet red, and my heart pounded out of its chest.

"Mr. Albert', my voice quivered, 'that was a silly quarrel and has no merit. You know Kerry and what a loose cannon he is."

"Yes, I'm painfully aware of that Patrick, but Brian wants to talk to you about it nonetheless. It doesn't sound too good for you, I'm afraid."

"Mr. Albert, please tell Brian about my grandmother and the money. I have to wait for my father's phone call which will be any moment now. In the meantime, you could explain all about Kerry and what he's like."

"Headquarters is very aware of Kerry's delinquent behaviors Patrick, he's facing severe sanctions. Both of you are, I'm sorry to say."

"I know Mr. Albert, but what's more important, a stupid little fight or hundreds of thousands of Dollars?" There was a long pregnant pause that suddenly turned awkward. Finally, Mr. Albert said: "You certainly do make a point there Patrick. I will discuss it right now with Brian. I will call you back."

"Thank you, Mr. Albert, I know that you will not let me down."

"Well, we can't let down the organization and the cosmic beings can we now Patrick?"

"No, Mr. Albert, they come first and thousands of people who will be converted to the cause as a result of this windfall." I gleefully blasphemed with an outstretched middle finger that pointed at the phone.

"You have a point, Patrick. I will call you straight away. I certainly will give it a try."

"Thank you, Mr. Albert, God bless you." I hung up the phone. I flipped him off in the process, but as I now recollect, I was flipping the whole damn den of thieves.

I was in a panic. If that Brian were to come to the Taylor's and get me, it would be all over. I decided that I couldn't take that risk. Jeff had already left for the meeting, so I was all alone in the house. Mrs. Taylor wasn't home yet. I flew down the steps into the basement and started packing all of my belongings as fast as I could. I thought if I get a head start I could be on the highway in no time, even though it was getting dark.

I gathered as much of my belongings as I could. I made as many trips back and forth and piled my belongings in the back of my trusty station wagon. It looked like a tornado had gone through it. I sweated profusely. I keep thinking that they were on their way to pick me up, which made the fear worse. My last trip to the station wagon was completed. I walked into the house for the last time, when I heard the phone ring! My heart skipped a beat. I timidly picked up the receiver and said, 'Hello Taylor's residence.' An unfamiliar husky voice said suddenly, "Yes, I would like to speak to Patrick McKallick."

"Yes, speaking," I said with a trembling voice.

"Patrick, this is Brian. I don't think that we have formally met, but Mr. Albert has told me about your family's situation."

"Yes sir, I'm anxious about my grandmother but very grateful for her generosity."

"Yes, Mr. Albert filled me in on all the details." Sweat poured from my forehead, and the hand that held the receiver was visibly shaking like a dry leaf in a robust autumnal wind.

"I have spoken with the TG just now, and it's clear to us that you should immediately follow your father's instructions and take care of your obligations."

"Yes sir, thank you, sir, you don't know what this means to me, and

I might add to the organization as well." He swiftly cut me off. "Don't delay, and the TG wants at least a monthly update as to your progress. You can call headquarters."

"Yes sir, I will."

"Oh, and reverse the charges, the call will be on us." He said cheerily.

"Oh, yes, of course, sir."

"Good luck Patrick, and good work."

"Thank you, sir!"

I breathed a big sigh of relief! I sank into Mrs. Taylor's wing back chair wholly exhausted as if I had been run over by a truck. I cried with happiness, I finally did it! I was going to be free at last. But I couldn't dally much longer. Either I leave right away, or I wait until the morning to start bright and early. I decided that departing in the morning would be too dangerous, especially if that Kerry decided to take revenge and do something stupid, like come over to the Taylor's and cause trouble. Or I thought, worst case scenario, the TG would become suspicious and order Brian to take me back to church headquarters for processing. I could not risk any one of those possibilities from taking place. So, I wrote notes to Jeff and Mrs. Taylor explaining to them that I had to catch a night flight to Mexico to attend to family business. I apologized profusely for not personally thanking them for all of their help, but I promised to be back soon, and I hoped they would understand.

I checked downstairs one last time for all of my belongings and got into my station wagon and drove away for the very last time! Fortunately, I had just received my latest paycheck and had cashed it, so I had about $250 to make the trip, which was plenty back in those days. I stopped at a gas station and bought a U.S. Atlas and plotted my course to head East and then South. I thought I would get a motel somewhere out of town. I could not wait to leave.

As I drove away, I thought about all the good friendships I had made, even though they were few in numbers. This caused me quite a bit of sadness. They were like my buddies in combat. I was abandoning them altogether, but nothing could surpass the exquisite joy of knowing that freedom was just to keep driving as far and as fast as I could. I thought to myself, each one must walk their own path. So, as I ponder these events and as I write these words, I'm chuckling. So, could I call this escape "Cultus Interruptus?" And I think that's precisely what it was! I was no longer going to get screwed over again. I would never allow myself to let other people do my thinking for me. There are those damn cursing entities still! Damn! I smiled to myself.

I drove about three hours and decided to call it a day. I checked into a decent motel off the main highway. I thought if they were going to follow me, my car would be out of sight from the main road. My paranoia was working overtime. I laid my head on the pillow, and I was gone to the world.

CHAPTER 5

THE YOUNG IGUANA

*"What we call the beginning is often the end.
And to make an end is to make a beginning.
The end is where we start from."*
~ T. S. Eliot

The next morning, I headed out of town across the northwest of the U.S. and eventually I joined the highways that led south to Texas where my sister and brother-in-law lived. The hot, dry wind had not let up, but the temperature was still morning-cooled, and so it made it a more comfortable drive. I dreaded the afternoon hours when the sun and the heat would be at their peak.

As I drove for two days, the barren desert of Northern Nevada offered nothing exciting to look at. It was annoyingly tedious. I had plenty of time to think about my situation. I often wondered why I would've joined a cult. Well, at first exposure, I didn't know it was a cult. That was my first mistake. Looking back, I don't even think I knew what a cult was or what it looked like. But the questions persisted. Why did I put myself in harm's way? Why did I surrender my spirit, my resources to thieves? Then my mind wandered to my childhood and everything that happened to me before this period in my life. As I was wearily driving through the hot desert, I remembered a particular incident in my childhood which stood out as clearly in my mind as if it had happened the day before.

The windswept rain beat heavily upon the 1930's art-deco glass windows. The lightning and thunder provided a brilliant light show of strobe lights, and our figures lit up as in slow motion ambling down the corridor. The power had gone out of course, as it generally does, especially in the rural areas of Mexico when it rains or when the wind suddenly blows. I was born there, and I grew up in a small, and beautiful colonial town in north-central Mexico. My grandparent's home was a large, red-tiled roof mansion that extended majestically and graciously upon a carefully coiffured garden, laboriously attended by the gardener, one of many employed by my grandparents. There was a spiral staircase made of exquisitely hand-crafted mosaic tiles, housed within a looming tower at the end of the long structure. It hovered auspiciously over beautifully kept blooms of bougainvillea's, roses and an assortment of other plants and tropical blossoms. The meticulously manicured gardens also harbored our pet "guacamaya," a rainbow-colored macaw whose wings were periodically trimmed to prevent its escape. When I was seven-years-old, my entertainment was to throw the animal up in the air. I got it to perch on our gardener's broomstick and up it went with enormous squawks. I would double over in laughter! My grandmother, Mamanita, violently tapped her knuckles on the cabana style windows to demonstrate her irritation at my cheap entertainment. She was not too pleased with my smart and unique pastime. But what did you expect from a seven-year-old kid?

My stepmother, Tere and I were hiding. We didn't have a light to guide us other than the intermittent strobe of lightning. She said to me hurriedly, 'Aquí, aquí, escóndete aquí' – 'Here, here, hide here' – I don't know what I would've done without her. She was a kind, considerate, loving woman who loved and cared deeply for my two sisters and me, and co-dependently for my vicious alcoholic father. We were fleeing from the unpleasant effects of one of his many raging binges. I hurried into an empty bedroom, and I slid under the bed. I wrapped a sheet around my body so that I would not be so readily identified should the electric power come back on. I also did that in case my father decided to heave his massive belly on the floor to search for me (I knew that would be most unlikely – but possible). My stepmother and I took a breather, and we chuckled as she stood by quietly. She whispered: "Why is it that everything happens all at once when it involves your father?"

She slid a couple of cigarettes at me and a box of matches, and she said: "Here, in case I take a while before I come back." I sighed with relief, knowing that I would have my nicotine fix if she took too long. Downstairs was way too quiet, and she worried that something may have happened to him. The darkness swallowed her as she felt her way down the spiral tiled staircase. Time passed slowly. I heard footsteps come up the stairs. My heart pounded, and I broke out into a sweat as I huddled under the bed.

Loud banging footsteps were always a source of high anxiety for me. When my father would get drunk, he would invariably come up to our bedrooms on the second floor to lecture us or scold us as we gagged at the smell of his disgusting alcohol breath. When my father drank, his voice got hoarser and deeper. At times, he would stomp his way up the terrazzo steps and yell out Patrick! Or any one of my sister's names. He trained us at an early age to answer him immediately when he called out to us and yell: "Yes Sir" or "Yes Daddy, coming!" If we didn't, there was hell to be paid.

When I first watched the movie *Mommie Dearest*, I almost had to leave the theatre. I felt like throwing up. I became so angered that I wanted to climb up on the screen and beat the crap out of Joan Crawford, (who was played by Faye Dunaway). My fantasy silently replaced her with my father. He would often come up and ask us a bunch of questions about our biological mother or did we really love him, or why didn't we do this or that, or why don't we behave, or he would just yell at us about some imagined lie we may have told. He hated anyone to lie to him. "Don't lie to me, don't lie to me, don't ever lie to me!" was our household motto.

I later figured out why he was paranoid about us lying to him. He fibbed most of the time himself! He lied to anyone that might oppose his collection of get-my-way-behaviors, especially his drinking. He evaded the truth and make up any story that would benefit him. Especially if it threatened his deep love affair with alcohol and/or with his alcoholic lifestyle. He was paranoid about his children even attempting to lie because he assumed everyone else lied the same way that he did.

The footsteps were careful and steady, and so I suspected that they belonged to my step-mother. Tere whispered loudly, "Patrick! You can relax - he fell asleep". I breathed a sigh of relief, crawled out from under the bed and unfurled the sheet from my slim body. I lit a cigarette, and we sat and talked about the evening. We processed our feelings, and we even had a good laugh, a laugh of relief and ease. My heart slowed down to a reasonable rhythm, and I could, at last, enjoy this private moment of peace.

These were examples of the many high-stress incidents that my sisters and I experienced. From hiding in motels with my biological mother before she divorced my father, to beatings and confrontations, to embarrassing moments in front of family and friends. One of my father's favorite tactics (and he had a toolbox full of these!) were to get drunk before dinner. When his cherished audience was assembled around the table, the harangue started. He had a captive audience, and my father loved every minute of it! It didn't matter if we had friends over visiting, or if my parent's friends came over, the show always got better the more members of the audience were present.

His harassment started with whoever was on his list that day, be it me, or one of my sisters. He was an expert at spoiling lunches and dinners or any reunion where the audience increased his pretense of grandiosity. These were just a sampling of incidents after incidents we experienced over the years. These were events that were accompanied by a pounding heart, sweaty palms, churning stomach and other fight/flight symptoms. Is it a wonder that I sought healing from the abuse? Is it a wonder that I looked in all the wrong places for any type of healing or reconciliation? Is it a wonder that I was able to survive years and years of this abuse and live to tell my story?

My father was my first teacher. I believe he was placed in my path so that I could learn humility and the sacredness of relationships and how important they are in our lives. By his mistreatment, he taught me to respect others and never mistreat them in any way, a lesson I'm still learning. He also showed me that violence is ugly and poisonous. But my father also taught me the value of forgiveness and compassion. He was a troubled man, a very sick man, mentally, physically, emotionally and spiritually. But the Divine spark in him showed that he was also a loving man. He cared for us and provided for us in the best way he knew how. At times, he was overly generous. I don't know if that came from guilt or to make up for the bad times, or if that was just his way of bribing us into forgiving him. At times, I couldn't help but feel his deep pain and torture.

My father was this giant glob of love, and fear, and hate, and caring and abuse. At times, it was just too much to bear. I overheard him say once to my stepmother: "Patrick really got the brunt of my anger." To this day I don't have a clue where that statement came from or in the context in which it was uttered. But, I do know now, that he was very conscious of the abuse he inflicted on me. I say that as a learner, not as a victim.

In life, our most valuable teachers are the ones who cause us the most pain. They are the teachers we've selected to teach our souls to grow and flourish. Paraphrasing Tony Robbins: "If he had been the father (in his case referring to his mother), I had wanted, I would not be the man I am proud to be." Dr. Michael Newton in his book <u>Journey of Souls: Case Studies of Life between Lives,</u> wrote: "If you had not been exposed to this person as a child, what would you now lack in understanding?" (Page 2971 Kindle version). That's an incredibly important question to ask ourselves. I have thought long and hard about that, and I sense my soul learned far more than my conscious mind has made me aware. But my conscious memory also tells me that by imposing fear on others through verbal or physical violence breaks all the bonds of human love and compassion. I sense that I have demonstrated my resilience as a human being and I have learned and grown in a way that is beyond my ability to explain to anybody, much less figure it out myself. My learning is found in my own inner knowing. I would like to think that I am by far a better person because of it.

I completely and entirely forgive my father and send him all of my total and complete unconditional love. I write these words with mixed feelings of anger and forgiveness. Assuming he was standing in front of me, I would resolutely say to him: "Without you, Dad, I don't think I would be writing these pages. Thank you, Dad, for teaching me what you did. Thank you for teaching me what fear can do to another human being. Thank you for giving me the insight to know that fear is a dangerous force. And furthermore, fear should never be instilled in another human being. Thank you for teaching me that power and control over other human beings are the cruel instruments of mental, and emotional slavery."

I have heard many authors and teachers, spiritual and otherwise, say that when it comes to hard or painful experiences we have to deal with in life, we are never given more than we can handle. I have, at times, found that hard to accept. But invariably, and in retrospect, I did survive the hard experiences, and it was as hard as I had thought it might have been, and in some cases, worse.

However, in all of my experiences, humor, has always come to my rescue. I believe that laughter is a universal healing energy that rejuvenates us and makes life bearable. I also think that humor is a spiritual energy that brings solace to our soul and heals our bodies. Dr. Raymond Moody discussed wit as an "anatomical and psychological mystery." Where does it come from? What is its basic nature? He says that, like many aspects of consciousness, it simply can't be explained. Charlie Chaplin said: "A day without laughter is a day that is wasted." And "there is little success where there is little laughter," wrote Andrew Carnegie. Norman Cousens stated in <u>Anatomy of an Illness</u> about how humor played a significant role in his healing.

So, I had many opportunities to laugh. Those moments of laughter were like oases in the desert. It was these memories that I resorted to in my darkest moments. Many humorous people and events in my life were like life rafts that would prove invaluable in the future when the oceans of life raged and became so violent and turbulent.

In addition to the memories of the pleasant and funny times, there was a series of life-changing teachings or bundles of information that managed to come into my conscious awareness, either directly or indirectly. These pieces of information served me and enlightened me and gave nourishment to my being. They helped me put the pieces of the puzzle together to help clarify why I had selected the road that I traveled. You may call the source of these pieces of information as coming from the "Still Small Voice" that I made reference to earlier.

I will intersperse these islands of respite throughout these pages in the hopes that you too will find them valuable. I suspect that you also will begin your inventory of the fun and refreshingly beautiful memories of your life and recognize these as your islands of joy and rest from the bad times, or the ugly memories and events that may have plagued your life.

The challenging events of my life seemed to have appeared in my life as if they were planned. I suspect the situations were indeed prepared by my soul with the assistance of an infinitely grander Universal Power. I believe we all came into this world with a plan for our life. Just because we drank out of the cup of amnesia before our appearance in this life, does not mean that it isn't real or meaningful. This now makes my journey so much more useful and with a profound sense of purpose, rather than just a fateful roll of the dice. More on this later.

CHAPTER 6

THE DESERT JOURNEY AFTER
THE DESERTED JOURNEY

*"Human extravagance has no bounds
when it comes to instilling fear."*
~ Dr. Michael Newton

*"Beliefs are big on earth. People collect them. Some
of these beliefs are helpful, but others just keep you
running around trying to follow rules that others have
laid down. They don't have a lot of personal meaning.
It's a good idea to sort through your beliefs now and
then and throw out the ones that don't serve you."*
~ Annie Kagan, The Afterlife of Billy Fingers.

I am hot and sweaty. I can only keep the window of my old 1968 Dodge station wagon opened just so much. The suffocating desert wind filled my smelly car with heat that was almost unbearable. From the first day I bought the thing, it had an odd, animal-like smell to it. Like a possum died in it or something like that. But I bought it anyway. What do you expect when you drive in the desert in an old car without air-conditioning? I bought this car because it was cheap and I was going off to study at *the school of infinite knowledge and light* to become "enlightened" or at least that's what I was lead to believe. I traveled at 70 miles an hour through the hot, barren desert of southern Arizona. I think to myself: "How could you have given up your nice late model air-conditioned car for this junky car?" Anger swelled up inside of me. How could I have been so gullible and accepting of lies and deceptions? How could I have given up my good paying job and exchanged it for all of this? At the same time, the thought of escaping from my prison-like doctrinal den sent a thrill through me. I was free! Or was I?

As I mentioned previously, I was going to call the cult leader "Top Iguana," but upon second thought, how could I possibly denigrate the iguanas of the world? They appear to have a bad rap anyway, why add to it? So, I called the leader "Top Guano." I suspected that guano was bat excrement, to later confirm that indeed that's precisely what it was. How appropriate! I also read that guano is one of the best fertilizers on the planet. I can identify with that as well, because it fertilized this work, making it available to all who may benefit from it. But I need to emphasize, as I attempt to practice the challenging virtue of compassion, that I choose to qualify only the lies that came out of the TG's mouth as guano. The putrid deceptions were merely that: lies. They sourced from the well of a sick mind – a deranged mind.

As to the person and persons who led the cult, I would like to thank all of them for helping me to become a better person. Again, quoting Tony Robbins' statement he gave in a major event he sponsored (referencing his mother): *"If she had been the mother I had wanted, I would not be the man I am proud to be."* And I can say the same: "If the TG had been the teacher I had wanted, I would not be the man I am proud to be today." Thank you for teaching me more about my own Divinity and

43

to honor and respect the Divinity that is within you. No matter the outward appearances or circumstances of anyone's life, our Divinity is an inviolate reality. However, its fundamental truth is not changed by beliefs or mental constructs. We are sparks of the Divine, sacred at the core of our being.

We have another sacrosanct aspect of our life that cannot be violated. And that is free will. It is sacred. I could've walked away from the cult but I didn't for many reasons. One of those being that I was thoroughly brainwashed and captured within the snares of their secret lies. But in the exercise of my free will, I stayed, and I have grown and become a better, more resilient human being. But I paid the price. I have also come to learn that those individuals were placed in my path for my own spiritual advancement, as was my father and all other human beings who challenged me and caused me pain. There was something that my Soul had to learn by going through those vile experiences. I believe that everyone who is placed in our path is there to teach us and help us grow as spiritual beings. So, if we are going to be compassionate, we must realize that our compassion is born out of gratitude for the learnings and growth that come from the difficult people in our lives. That can be a tough pill to swallow.

As the Joshua trees flew past my side windows and as the sun-scorched Arizona mountains loomed in the distance, I thought to myself, what would I do if I broke down in the middle of the desert? Surely someone would come to my rescue. I pushed that thought aside as I did all the other fearful notions of the so-called forces of darkness. More cultic regurgitations were making themselves visible to my consciousness. I pushed those thoughts aside and kept saying to myself: "Patrick, your attention, your attention! Stop thinking that way!" I devised an incredible array of techniques and methods and tricks to distract my mind and keep the iguana in check. Sometimes it worked, and other times it didn't, and my experiences became flashback nightmares so familiar with PTSD.

I very much identify with the quote by Cheryl Strayed: "Fear, to a great extent, is born of a story we tell ourselves." I was telling myself so many stories. But the problem was not the stories themselves, but my belief that those stories were actually real when in reality, they were the complete opposite. But the iguana was there, nevertheless, hidden and in many ways very ready to strike at any moment.

I was on my way to Texas. My family was living there and hopefully, I could stay with them until I could get a job. I had called them and told them that I was finally "coming home." The lost prodigal son, brother, brother-in-law, uncle, friend, acquaintance, he was finally coming home from being lost in the jungle of specters and monsters! The one who had graduated from college only 5 years before. It was later that I found out that my family was trying to find out how they could get me out of that "church." My sister even went to see her parish priest. I don't know what he told her. But the point is that it seemed hopeless to both of them, indeed a lost cause.

I remember one time, just before I moved to the house along the coast, I was in a supermarket, and I had an incredible longing to hear my family's voices. I felt like the drifting seaman who had to abandon ship and was all alone in a tempestuous sea on the brink of a cruel and fatal drowning. It was strictly prohibited to call one's family because they would dissuade one to abandon the church. So, I got the courage to call them anyway, and I stuck a handful of quarters in the pay phone and anxiously dialed their number in Texas. It rang, and rang, and rang. My heart dropped and tears of longing and sadness sprouted from my bloodshot eyes as the quarters noisily dumped into the coin return. At that time, there were no voice call recorders. I couldn't leave a message. But besides that, what number would they call me back at? I felt lonely and abandoned and very depressed.

I spent the night in an old run down, but clean motel. But it was air-conditioned! The loud, ancient window unit shook the walls of the room when it cycled on and off. The puddles of water outside streaked the cement walkway with the green slime of a constant flow of condensation. I thought that the owners of the old motel didn't care how the place looked, which seemed to add to its strange rustic charm.

I took a long refreshing shower and then headed out to get something to eat. I walked into a well-populated diner and sat down at an empty table next to raggedly looking semi drivers who couldn't stop talking about their trucks and their truck parts. At least they weren't talking about their old worn out body parts, natural or otherwise! I had to listen to their annoying stories. But at the same time, I found solace being among the *ordinary* people, who weren't talking about cosmic beings and the karma that would befall mankind if they didn't repent, and all that bullshit! I had forgotten how regular people looked, spoke, and behaved. It felt I had just gotten out of a concentration camp and I was stupefied by the normalcy around me. I really did feel like an alien that had just traveled from a far away galaxy and just landed to witness this bizarre scene. However, it felt good! It felt liberating, but it felt oddly threatening and scary at the same time.

I had skimpy choices available from the down-home truckstop menu. I had not only been a convert to falsehoods but also I was pressured into vegetarianism. But that didn't last long. So, I ordered vegetables that were overcooked with lumpy mashed potatoes. "Aren't you going to have any meat hon?" asked the snaggletooth waitress as she breathed out the stench of the last cigarette she had smoked. The smell was so putrid it could've charmed a vulture off a rotting corpse.

Declining politely, I turned my head as to not catch the rest of her stale breath. She sensuously wagged her behind away from my table in front of the truckers, probably in hopes of snatching the attention of at least one of them. I thought to myself that she must've heard that the 18 wheelers had very cushiony sleeping cabins and she was aching to fill one, well accompanied, of course. The thought disgusted me. I pretended to read a book I had brought along. But I couldn't concentrate on the words in the pages. I was too captivated and at the same time, quite terrified of this strange new environment that I found myself in, after all, what do you say and do when you find yourself in such an odd setting? How do you act so that you don't draw unwanted attention to yourself? I could just hear the waitress tell her co-workers: "See that kid over there, he didn't order any meat! Just vegetables! Must be one of *them* California health freaks."

I gobbled up my food as quickly as I could and paid my bill. I jumped in my trustworthy Dodge station wagon and left for my musty but welcoming hotel room. I crawled into bed drained, mentally, emotionally, and physically from all of the strange new events of that long dry day. As I was drifting away to sleep, I thought how I was going to explain the cult thing to my family. My shame and embarrassment lulled me to sleep.

CHAPTER 7

FROM EMERGENCY TO EMERGENCE

"A hero is someone who understands the responsibility that comes with his freedom."
~Bob Dylan

I arrived back in Texas. My family was glad to see me. It had been 8 years since I had seen them, and like being in a Gulag, I had no communication with them at all or with anyone, for that matter. That is one of the traits of cults, as I mentioned before, first rules for captured members: "You are strictly forbidden to contact your families." We were told that if we contacted our families, we would be subjected to "family hypnotism" and we would succumb to their hypnotic persuasion to abandon the "cause." The other party line was that the would-be dark forces would put a spell on the family and on me to divert me from the *light*. The only hypnotic trance came from the TG and its lieutenants of insanity.

It was awkward at first. I didn't know what to say. Where did I go wrong? Why did I do a stupid thing like that? I was grateful and relieved that they were restrained in asking too many questions. My sister told me she was distraught, as was my other sister and needless to say, my mother as well. No amount of concern for my well-being would get me back. But here I was. I tried to avoid further questioning as much as possible. Changing the subject came in very handy, and I got very good at it. I desperately wanted to put that awful chapter of my life behind me. My only chance of reintegrating myself within the normality of life, that everyone lived, was to live exactly as everyone else lived. I needed to think like everyone else did, as a rational human being. After all, the cultists were the insane ones. I had to return to sanity and normality.

The efforts of reintegration into society were lonely and fastidious. To this day, I don't know where I got the courage and fortitude to adapt to such a drastic new way of life. But I kept telling myself that I had done this before and it was just a matter of more effort and strength to return to where I had started. But it was an uphill battle. Part of the integration process was abandoning vegetarianism. Then, I returned to drinking alcohol (frequently to excess) and smoking cigarettes. There! I was now *ordinary*, I said, proudly to myself. Now, I could go look for a job and really make a nice living for myself. I did just that.

Since I had been working in the criminal justice system before my adventure into the wild blue insanity of cultism, I applied for a Probation Officer position. My experience and my bilingualism smoothly landed me the job. I was thrown into the most chaotic role I had ever experienced. I was assigned 200, needle sticking, polydrug abusing probationers, and I only had one assistant to help me. There were no computers in those days, and the documentation of office visits, field visits, court appearances, violation reports all had to be done longhand to be handed over to secretaries to type up. I never caught up. The files were stacked mercilessly on my desk begging for attention, actually, screaming for attention. I could almost hear them yelling at me "if you don't mind me, I will tattle tell on you." The bureaucracy was overwhelming. The snakes in the organization laid in wait ready to strike. And it seemed they were after me.

I had one good friend, who I went to college with, who kept an eye out for me. "Patrick, if you don't cover your ass, they're talking about firing you." She got my attention. I couldn't afford that. I had bought a new car, small though it was, it was still a luxury that I couldn't afford to be without. I couldn't be fired. So, I doubled up on my reluctant investment in the job with the greatest of distaste and resolve, but only to keep the meager income at the time. I was desperate to find something better.

After a year of struggling, I got the word, in a very round-about way, of a job as a program monitor in a state agency. I applied as soon as I could and got the job! I couldn't have been happier to leave. My new job was a relief, but not without its usual problems, including problematic people. Navigating around organizational precipices has never been one of my fortes. If there is anything that makes me wild is the fact that in any vast bureaucracy you have to be on your toes and not step on the wrong ones. This was never easy for me. My immediate supervisor was one whom you didn't step on. She at first was friendly and accommodating and then, in a flash, turned into an ogre and a witch.

Although I had to deal with her, the job kept me on the road all over the state, and it kept me far away from her sufficiently to make it bearable. I also attended conferences and conventions on the subject of my employment, and many of those were in cities in other states. I liked the travel and the diversity. During the last year at that job, I had the opportunity to work with our counterparts in Mexico. I became the liaison between our agency and the institution for drug prevention in Mexico. Frequent trips to Mexico and the border were monthly. I had the opportunity to go home on several of those trips. That was something that I had not expected. I stayed at that job for about 4 years.

As with any job, change seems to be around the corner, especially in my younger years. I was recruited by the director of a Regional Training Center of the U.S. Department of Education. It was, by far, the most rewarding job that I ever had. The second most rewarding professional work was as a private consultant in International training and development. I worked steadily for approximately fifteen years as an independent consultant and trainer for the various international agencies such as the U.S. Agency for International Development, the U.S. State Department, the Organization of American States (OAS), and many non-governmental organizations. My final long-term job was working with the criminal justice system as a Cognitive Behavioral Counselor. However, it was at the Training Center that I acquired the first prominent wealth of information that not only helped me to develop my innate talents and gifts but helped me to understand myself and my background better.

The regional training center provided a prolific period of growth and learning for me. I found out that I was a good trainer, and more importantly that I excelled at adult education and developed a real passion for it. This would follow me for the rest of my professional life. I also came in contact with the most impressive group of human beings that I had ever been in contact with, and with whom I shared a genuine passion for excellence in training and education. I traveled throughout the 10 states in the Southwest of the United States and participated in many international conferences, mainly along the border. It was perhaps the best on-the-job-education I have ever received. One of the most critical pieces of information that inspired the discovery of the potential reasons for having joined a destructive cult would unfold at this juncture in my life.

CHAPTER 8

"HAVE YOU SEEN RUTHIE?"

"I believe that imagination is stronger than knowledge. That myth is more potent than history. That dreams are more powerful than facts. That hope always triumphs over experience. That laughter is the only cure for grief. And I believe that love is stronger than death."
~Robert Fulghum

In life, we are given many opportunities to learn. The situations we are experiencing are essential for our development both spiritually and physically. We are many times lost without having a sense of direction on the wind tossed surf that rocks the ship of our being. Then, suddenly and without warning, a beautiful island appears on the horizon, and then we contemplate an upcoming rest from the tempestuous seas of life. These islands were those moments of discovery and wonderment. One such finding that answered many of my questions was the Opposite Strengths program (and many others) that I will share later. But, islands of respite are also the rich life experiences that Spirit (I refer to Spirit as the alternate for the worn out word God) gives us to rest our weary souls. In this case, it is the memory of the happy times, the funny times, and the people that inhabit our treasure trove of fun-filled recollections.

The Universe seems to be saying to us, *Let's take a rest and breathe the peace that surrounds us*. And then we breathe in the solace of eternal love as it glides into our being and our essence. Oh, happy memories! They are thick in design and rich in texture, and they weave a beautiful tapestry of our Soul's plan for this lifetime. What do we have to look forward to in our life? The happy times and the times of rest and relaxation.

Going back to my initial trip across the desert in my 1968 Dodge, I recalled one of the most impacting stories of my family that to this day brings joy and contentment to my heart. These are, but a few of the stories or events in my life that I can literally say made the journey in the desert bearable.

One of my most significant sources of laughter was my paternal grandmother. Her name was Anita, but everyone called her Mamanita. She was a beautiful woman. Mamanita was a unique character. She made my sisters, family, and I laugh a lot. She made everyone laugh. And the funny thing is she didn't mean to be humorous she was just plain hilarious by nature. My teenage years were a particularly difficult time for me as well as my sisters due to my father's alcoholism. But it seemed like Mamanita was always there to come to the rescue and lighten things up. Mamanita was jovial, loving, caring, charming, and almost graciously clumsy, with a savvy and keen sense of innate intelligence.

My grandfather, on the other hand, was more inflexible and extremely organized. His handwriting was sculpted and molded to perfection. He was the envy of any calligrapher. My grandmother was the total opposite. She was delightfully messy, and her mess invited mirth from all of those inquisitive personalities in her sphere of come-what-may lifestyle. She violated any orders from my grandfather that she could, such as *Nita don't drink too much; Nita, don't spend so much money; Nita hurry up we have to leave.*

When my grandparents would have a gathering with their friends, invariably, she quietly invited all of her lady friends to join her in her large walk-in closet to view her latest fashions, dresses, shoes, a bottle of booze and plenty of cigarettes. The party suddenly transferred, unbeknownst to anybody, to Mamanita's walk-in closet, a marvelous invention in those days. How did that suddenly happen without anybody knowing about it? Only Mamanita could excel at making that occur seamlessly and flawlessly. My sisters would hide under the bed and listen to the jokes and the laughter and smell the cigarette smoke as it flowed out from under the closed closet door. They knew how to entertain themselves at Mamanita's expense. Mamanita knew how to amuse everybody, without even knowing it. But she was also very talented. She frequently organized Canasta parties with her friends. She loved to gamble and made sure her friends were well served during these events. Although she did enjoy her "copitas," (cocktails in Spanish), she held back a bit during her games to be sure she would win the pot more often than not!

My grandparents had a summer home in Acapulco, and it was right across the street from one of the more popular beaches on the Bahia de Santa Lucia. Acapulco was a haven for us, even though it was very far from our home in northern Mexico. We spent most of our summers there, and it seemed like my father was more calm and moderate in his drinking. I particularly loved to go swimming twice a day. We had a float that we used to surf the waves. At the house, we would listen to my father's old 33's – *in Living Stereo* of course! We listened to Frank Sinatra, Louis Armstrong, his favorite, and the Mills Brothers. Summer Wind by Frank Sinatra was my favorite and every time I hear it, the memories of those beautiful tropical memories joyfully flood my mind. I remember the smell of Alberto VO5, and when I took a whiff of that now rare hair styling gel, I would immediately be transported back to my high school years, fun summer times, and the tropical beauty of Acapulco.

One Summer, one of my uncles called my dad and my grandfather and said in a panic: "You got to help me, Ruthie has run away with Chris. She is on the S.S. Oriana that is sailing for Southampton. You have to get her off that ship." Ruthie was my adorable, fun loving first cousin who had fallen in love with a tall, good-looking Brit whom she adored. So, my father and my grandfather rushed off to get permits from the port authority to board the ship and extract my cousin Ruthie from the departing liner.

Meanwhile us 3 kids, actually 2 teenagers and a pre-teen, were babysitting Mamanita. Needless to say, Mamanita was in a terrible state. She kept wringing her hands and pacing back and forth muttering: "Oh Ruthie! Oh, Ruthie! What have you done! Why did you go away with him?" Then as quickly as she said that, she gleefully turned to us with a very naughty smile on her face and blurted out: "Well I think I would have done the same, Chris is a very handsome young man, don't you think so girls?" My sisters nodded in agreement. But, as soon as the words were spoken, she shot up from her comfortable chair and returned to her routine of pacing and wringing her hands. "Why haven't they called us? Why aren't they telling us they got her off the ship?" and she paced, and paced, and paced, and then we noticed that she would suddenly dash off to her bedroom. When she re-emerged back into the living area, we saw that she was remarkably more relaxed and, oddly, a distinct glassy look adorned her matronly gaze. I looked at my older sister, and we both knew what she was up to. It was not uncommon for her to have a stash of booze in her bedroom hidden away from my grandfather's scrutinizing inspection. He disapproved, of course, unless it was he who partook, sometimes to excess, especially after his golf games with his buddies.

Finally, at around 3 PM, Mamanita had enough of waiting and boozing. She suddenly and ceremoniously announced, after many intoxicating excursions to her bedroom: "I'm going down to that ship, and I am getting my granddaughter off that ship myself, those dumb men don't know what the hell they're doing."

"No Mamanita, they won't let you on the ship you have to have special permission," we pleaded.

"Oh? Yes, they will! They don't know who they are dealing with!!"

The flavored whiskey words shot out of her mouth like drunken arrows. So, at 3:30, we all piled into an old, musty Acapulco taxi. We arrived at the dock where the tenders were ferrying last-minute passengers back to the S.S. Oriana that was readying for her 5 pm scheduled departure out of Acapulco Bay.

No amount of arguing by Mamanita was going to convince the British officers, in their crisp tropical whites, that Ruthie was a top priority and she had to be rescued.

"Mamanita, please, they are not going to let anybody on board who is not a passenger," I begged.

"Oh, yes they will, they don't know who the hell they are dealing with!" she yelled with feigned anger that we always laughed at because we knew she wasn't mad. Mamanita had to make her point, and she often did when it meant something significant and dear to her. She allowed a pregnant pause to let her last statement sink into our young minds.

After her increasingly defiant insistence, the ship's officers firmly told Mamanita, like only a well-bred Brit could, that, in so many polite words she was to *F-off*. I loved the way they so politely motioned to people to go *F-themselves* without them actually pronouncing the word, but firmly uttering words with the same meaning and intent!!! I thought it was brilliant and really admired that trait in them. I guess that's why I love to watch anything British. Who could live without Masterpiece Theatre?!

Finally, she gave up. She muttered words in Spanish at the officers: "Váyanse por un tubo," the Spanish equivalent for: "Go flush yourselves down a toilet!" I thought, finally, she got the message, and we could go home now! She couldn't go to the ship and get her granddaughter off. That was the end of that. There was no further arguing the matter. But how terribly wrong I was. My darling Mamanita wasn't going to let the issue be settled by some cocky Brit sailor who thought that nobody could sink his boat.

So, she took the flask of booze out of her purse and gulped downed a quick swig as if garnering more courage and determination to finish the task. In no time flat, she was off to barter with an old fisherman sitting in a boat how much he would charge for a trip to the liner. The ancient craft kept bumping against the dock in sync with the waves of the bay, and it looked like it was about to sink to the bottom of Acapulco Bay. Mamanita negotiated the charge with the fisherman, and they finally agreed on a price. We didn't want to go and pleaded with her to abandon the idea.

"No way!" she belted out, "I'll go myself, and you don't have to go with me. They'll let me on the ship." "No Mamanita, it's not going to work," we screamed in unison.

Mamanita had a curious habit that when she got really nervous, her tongue would dart in and out like a snake stuck on fast forward, smelling for the next prey to devour. So, we all piled very carefully into this old, sorry excuse for a boat. I was furious! How could this old lady, my dear, darling grandmother, suddenly commandeer all of us, literally, out to sea? She hijacked us without so much as firing a single shot! So off we went to the big white ship anchored in the middle of Acapulco Bay. I sat next to the loud, smoky, uncovered ancient outboard motor. The filthy little boat rocked back and forth, and it was challenging for Mamanita to coordinate the docking of her Whiskey flask to her mouth! So, it was one wave following the other. Her hand clenched the vial for dear life and waved it up and down in synch with the waves like a conductor conducting an orchestra. Finally, her mouth found the opening of the container, and quickly she tipped it. Down the hatch, the booze went, with a big gulp and a quick, lip-smacking smile.

After fifteen minutes of rocking and rolling and many precarious swigs of whiskey, we finally arrived at the towering ocean liner. In the early 1960's, the S.S. Oriana was a vast white ship of the P&O Lines out of Southampton, and the ultimate in ocean travel. Mamanita ordered the fisherman, like a confident captain of her own little boat, to circle the ship. The fisherman looked at her like she wasn't rowing with both oars in the water. As we orbited the floating giant, Mamanita looked up at the crowded railings and yelled at the top of her voice:

"Ruthie, Ruthie, where are you, Ruthie? please don't go, Ruthie!"

Passengers lined up, looking down at amazement at this old lady and 3 kids in this rickety old boat and pointed at as if we were rare marine specimens. Mamanita periodically yelled out to them: "Have you seen Ruthie? Please tell her to come home! Have you seen Ruthie?" "Have you seen Ruthie?" I buried my face in my hands I was so overcome by embarrassment. We circled the ship like a voracious shark waiting for the attack on an unsuspecting victim.

Five PM arrived right on schedule and little did we know that that was Oriana's scheduled departure time. The ship's horn thundered its adios to Acapulco 3 times, and we just happened to be at the bow of the vessel when the clanking of the massive anchor chain made a deafening racket that scared us almost to the point of capsizing the already unsteady boat. Mamanita yelled in Spanish at the indigenous captain of the fishing vessel: "Let's get the hell out of here!" Only the word in Spanish in no way came close to hell in English. It was a bit more crusty, to put it mildly. So off we went back to the dock, and Mamanita's tongue darted in and out like crazy in between swigs of booze and crying: "Oh Ruthie, oh Ruthie!" She uttered Ruthie's name in a sad but resolved manner, "Well at least she'll have a good time with that boyfriend of hers! Oh! Those were the days," she muttered with a faraway stare at the horizon. Her troubled face suddenly looked exhausted and depleted. I felt sorry for my dear grandmother.

It happened that when we arrived back at the house, exhausted and sweaty and reeking of fish and motor oil, we were greeted by my grandfather, father, and none other than Ruthie herself in all her glory. Mamanita screamed! She cried and flung herself into Ruthie's arms. She told her that she was so happy she was safe. Almost in the same breath, she blurted out: "Why did you do it hon?" Ruthie answered very determinedly and with a slight quiver in her voice: "Ay Mamanita, ya sabes porque!" "You know why! Because I love him and I want to marry him, and I am going to marry him."

My grandfather looked down at her disapprovingly. My cousin Ruthie was my favorite of all my cousins because she didn't bow down to her parent's strict rules. I loved her rebelliousness and envied her daringness to speak her mind, no matter the outcomes. I always wanted to emulate her and tell a few of my own family members what part of hell they could park their asses. Then Mamanita reached over and patted Ruthie on her beautiful, but disheveled ash brown hair. "Ay chula (honey) don't worry you'll get married when you're supposed to."

"But I want to marry him now because I can't be without him not even a minute," she pouted and broke down into tears. Mamanita swaddled Ruthie in her generous bosom and blurted out: "Don't cry hon, you know I would've done the same thing, and I probably would never have ever come back!' Mamanita then took another swig of her golden elixir as my grandfather voiced his disapproval 'You've had enough Nita!' With a swift wave of her hand, she blurted: "What does that amigo know" she looked at us voicing her contempt for my grandfather's chastisement.

To lighten things up, Mamanita seemed to announce to all of us present: "You know why I never became a nun don't you?"

"No Mamanita why?" we all chanted in unison knowing what was coming. And with a sly wicked smile on her face, she said: "Because then I couldn't get none." And she roared at her own joke as we all did. But we laughed more at her laughing at her own joke and the fact that she would always forget that she'd had told that one many an occasion. But we, nonetheless, laughed at that one for many years to follow.

My aunt, Ruthie's mother, said that she could go to England and be with Chris if she was so in love with him, but only on the condition that they were to be married. In a phone conversation between Ruthie, her parents, and Chris and his parents, they all agreed that it would be in the best interest of all involved that Ruthie and Chris should marry. Ruthie left for England and was wed to Chris in a grand ceremony. They lived in England for five years. Ruthie and Chris were desperately in love. Ruthie would tell me years later and not terribly long before her death, that it was unbearable to live without the love of her life, her soul mate. She felt she had known him for all eternity. Her marriage was joyful and produced two beautiful girls who were born in Mexico after their return. I've never seen two people so deeply in love. Ruthie was eager to get back to her roots as well and to show off her dashing beau to her friends and family. They should've stayed in Great Britain. Mexico proved tragic to their loving bond.

CHAPTER 9

MAMANITA AND CHRIS: MIRTH AND TRAGEDY

"A well-developed sense of humor is the pole that adds balance to your steps as you walk the tightrope of life."
~William Arthur Ward

"The tragedy is not that love doesn't last. The tragedy is the love that lasts."
~Shirley Hazzard

THE MIRTH

Mamanita was notorious for her antics. She gave everybody the impression that she was oblivious to everything happening around her, a bright delusion that she wove for everyone to see. She had a hearing aid and did have difficulty hearing. Frequently, she complained that her hearing aid, either wasn't working right, or the batteries had gone down. Sometimes, I think that she did this on purpose. I believe that because those around her would spill valuable information that she would later use to her own advantage. For instance, she would find out how much cash my grandfather had available for withdrawal at the large truck and car dealership they owned. She would then get my father to withdraw amounts sufficient not to arouse suspicion but enough that she could buy vacant lots and houses.

When she was visiting Mexico City, she concentrated her purchases in the up and coming fancy suburb, of Mexico City known as the Lomas de Chapultepec or also known by the expats as *The Heights*. She bought, unbeknownst to my grandfather, a small fortune in houses and lots at low prices. The Depression had hit Mexico hard, and my grandfather's business was affected, but it managed to survive in spite of the economic downfall. So Mamanita took advantage of the depressed economy. She bought low and sold high. This came in handy when eventually she or my grandfather would need it toward the end of their days.

Mamanita had a habit of visiting the Lagunilla Market in Mexico City. It was also known as the Thieves Market. She loved antiques of any kind and had an eye for what was valuable and what wasn't. She had her contacts in the market, and when an exceptional piece would come in that they thought she would be interested in, they called her to let her know. They often reserved the article, just in case she was interested in it. She was known as *La Señora Doña Anita*, loosely translated as *the very respected Mrs. Anita*. She bought and bought and bought. She filled up empty rooms of her large, sprawling colonial house in the countryside. She even had a storage room constructed on her property to be filled with beautiful, probably stolen, antique furniture and artifacts.

My grandfather would have veritable meltdowns every time a delivery truck would arrive unannounced at their house to drop off truckloads of furniture.

"Nita, what in the holy hell is all this crap?"

"Did you buy all this?"

The Doña Anita kept her cool.

"As a matter of fact, Robert, yes I did!" "So, what?"

My grandfather's face was a beet red compared to his otherwise white as snow semblance. It was useless to argue with her, and he knew that after sixty or so years of marriage.

In the long run, she had the last laugh, figuratively and literally as this treasure would come in handy when money was needed in their final days. Grandpa transitioned first followed by Mamanita five years later. Some of these priceless antiques we inherited as she finally crossed over from this life.

Mamanita was seemingly as innocent as a mouse. She feigned ignorance and absent-mindedness while at the same time she was plotting her next move. She would scour the newspapers for houses or lots for sale. She would then call my grandfather to send a chauffeur from the dealership to come pick her. She conjured many excuses why she had to get out of the penthouse where they lived on the glamorous Reforma Boulevard in cosmopolitan Mexico City. She ordered the driver to drive to all kinds of places she had discovered in the newspaper to check out potential bargains, sometimes stopping to discuss prices with the owners.

Mamanita made sure that her intrepid adventures into Mexican real estate were not discovered by my grandfather. So, she would be extra friendly with the chauffer reminding him that he would always be well taken care of. She was generous in exchange for his silence. Mamanita would never call this a bribe. Heavens no! This was a bonus for taking care of her and of course, his absolute discretion: "Si Señor, llevé a su Señora esposa al salón de belleza," "Yes sir, I drove your wife, the Señora, to the hair salon."

My dear grandmother appeared to be absent-minded, and many times she was. But overall, she was a very elegantly intelligent and cunning woman whose main camouflage was looking ignorant and not in touch with the world around her when in fact it was just the opposite.

Her astuteness in her real estate purchases was astounding. When the Great Depression arrived in Mexico, her real estate investments and other surreptitious acquisitions, like land and precious antiques and other valuables, saved my grandfather's business from going down like the ill-fated Titanic.

In the mid-1920's, I can't remember what year precisely, she was determined to have her own independence and not have to rely so much on the chauffeurs who might betray her to the *patrón*, my grandfather. She desperately wanted to go where she pleased when she pleased. So, she decided that she was going to learn how to drive her own vehicle. That didn't sit so well with my grandfather, but as usual, she won out after dogged insistence. With that, she took driving lessons, and Mamanita became one of the first women drivers in Mexico City. Mexican men, in all their macho glory, were not very happy with women who drove cars. That was a man's business, and women didn't need to be meddling in men's affairs, like maneuvering big fancy cars in the complicated streets of the big metropolis.

Mamanita told me many times that when she drove, and men honked their horn at her for no reason, it infuriated her. She frequently honked her horn back and with a wave of her delicate hand prominently display her middle finger at them. And then she giggled with much delight. My sisters and I laughed when she laughed, especially at her own one-liners. The picture and sound of her giggles are as real to me now as they were then. She seemed to love to tell, especially the male sex, to go take a hike. But it wasn't restricted to the male sex. She'd go after anyone else that got in the way of her plans.

The other tidbit about Mamanita that I have always found amusing was that every time she'd come to the railway crossings in Mexico, she would honk her horn. At that time in Mexico, railroad crossing did not have electronic gates or lights or warnings. According to her, honking her horn would be sufficient to let the train know that it was to stop when she crossed the tracks! To this day, I just can't seem to understand how she never had an accident! I am sure her team of Guardian Angels had their hands full keeping her safe. I'm sure they were also quite entertained with her antics!

Mamanita was a woman of complete unpredictability. We never

knew when she would drop another surprise bomb, seemingly out of thin air. I remember the story of my sister who was pregnant with her first child. Mamanita told my sister before the baby was born, "Well it sure went in easy, didn't it?!" And of course, that brought the house down! My sister laughed as well, how could anyone avoid it! Shortly afterward she had a beautiful baby girl.

Mamanita didn't pay too much attention to what was going on around her, unless, it was something exciting or to her benefit. And even though her hearing aid was working fine, at times, she pretended she didn't hear. But, nevertheless, was busy collecting valuable data and information for her next schemes. But, I can't deny that she was not absent-minded. She was. But, I think a lot of times she was far too occupied worrying about this or that or taking inventory of her many acquisitions.

Her inattentiveness was frequent and at time pronounced. For instance, she lighted one cigarette and put it in the ashtray. In no more than 30 seconds she lit another cigarette and put that one in the ashtray. We said to her: "Mamanita you have 2 cigarettes!" "Oh, I do?" She also had a habit of chewing gum. But she often forgot that she already had a piece of gum in her mouth. At times, she would have a massive lump of 3 or 4 sticks of gum at once. When we were seated at the dining table for lunch, we would pass around the silver bread tray. Invariably, and almost like clockwork, the silver bread tray carried with it a very important passenger in the form of one big enormous lump of glossy and wet chewing gum for everyone to admire. It was especially embarrassing when we had guests for lunch. One of us would quickly snap the bread tray from Mamanita and rescue her lump of gleaming chewing gum from the plate with a swift slight of the hand. That included a quick wipe off of the saliva!

On one occasion, we were all sitting very politely in a fancy up-market Mexico City restaurant. Mamanita had just downed her 2 *copitas* (or cocktails in Spanish). The more she drank, the louder she got. Not hearing very well herself, even when she was sober, she had a hard time measuring the right volume of her voice. She glanced around the room, and her eyes rested on this very homely looking woman not too far from our table. Very noisily she announced to everyone who could hear her: "Oh look at that woman!" and we glanced over at the direction she was pointing. My step-mother Tere, with an uncontrollable smile, said: "Mamanita! eso no se hace!" "You don't do those things!" Mamanita quickly darted off her usual response with a wave of her hand. She then said in a very solemn voice: "Poor thing! Oh, poor thing!" she paused for effect and then yelled: "She is SO UGLY!" Well, we could not contain ourselves. I felt like crawling under the table with a mixture of embarrassment and amusement. I told my step-mom: "I think the lady heard us." She acknowledged what we knew to be true. But we left the restaurant as if nothing had happened and, for additional effect, we acted as if we were terribly bored. But once we got in the car, all of us, including my dad and my grandfather, could not contain ourselves. We laughed and joined in commenting on how hideous the woman really was!

Mamanita always accused my father and my grandfather of rushing her to get ready to go wherever we were supposed to go. That made her absolutely crazy! If there were a place that we had to go, either one of them would entrust us with checking up on her progress and urge her to get ready. She protested vehemently. One time we were late for an event. We practically ended up pushing Mamanita out of the door and out of the main gate of her house where my father and grandfather impatiently waited with the motor running. Mamanita had her exquisitely embroidered mantilla delicately placed on her silvery mane. One of my sisters held her arm to help her negotiate the steep incline of the driveway. Suddenly, and without warning, she screamed at the top of her voice: "I didn't put any panties on!!!" We just shook our heads in amazement and amusement. Only Mamanita would come up with that one. My sister would later confirm that; indeed, she hadn't put any panties on!

Remembering Mamanita and her outrageous behaviors and her incredible sense of humor helped me get out of some depressing periods of my life. During the desperate and dark days of my physical and mental captivity in the cult, I would relive these experiences in my mind. These memories brought a smile to my face and gave me a glimmer of hope that one day I would return to my days of laughs and happiness and more importantly, to the safety of Mamanita and home. I knew in my heart that I would escape the insane grasp of that deranged cultist's sick mind. Many a time I imagined Mamanita reaching out to me and smiling and tell me that everything was going to be OK. I felt she had a particular fondness for all her grandchildren. Her distant, but seeming nearby presence was very tangible. After a year and a half of captivity, Mamanita helped me escape from the clutches of the prisoners who held me captive. However, she never knew, even to the day of her death, that she helped me escape. She knows now though.

So, we are given trials, and we are given islands of respite to renew our souls. Mamanita was one of those resting islands for me. The same was true for my step-mother, Tere (short for Teresa), who really was the principle mother figure in my life and who raised my sisters and me. They both encouraged me and gave me emotional and spiritual sustenance, both in their own individual and different way. I don't know what I would've done without either one of them.

THE TRAGEDY

You may ask what exactly happened to Chris, Ruthie's husband? My aunt and uncle had a modest beach house in a small port city in the state of Veracruz. Chris was able to get an excellent job in Mexico working for my grandfather and uncle. Their two beautiful daughters were five and a half, and the younger one was four years old. Chris and Ruthie kept mostly to themselves and occasionally would participate in family outings.

On a dreary day late in October, Ruthie suggested that they accept my aunt and uncle's invitation to spend a long weekend at their place on the beach. Ironically, it was the weekend of the Day of the Dead or El Día de Los Muertos which is highly celebrated in Mexico. They eagerly agreed as they desperately wanted to escape from the doldrums of the big city.

As I recall Ruthie's narration of the flow of events, Chris and one my first cousins and some friends of his, decided to go fishing at the spot where a large river emptied into the Gulf of Mexico. Chris liked to build things, and one of those was a boat that he wanted to take out for a test run. The weather in November on the Gulf of Mexico can be unpredictable and tricky. Chris and my cousin took the boat out for their adventure in the choppy and murky waters of the Gulf. As they were out exploring the waters of the sea, a sudden storm capsized their boat. They swam as best as they could against strong currents and winds. They came upon a sandbar where they were able to rest, but Chris couldn't go any further as he was totally exhausted. He told my cousin and his friends to get help as the shore was not too far away. My cousin said that he would be right back for him and Chris yelled out to him with a big smile "Cheers! I'll be here when you get back!"

They returned with help a half hour later, and Chris was nowhere to be found. They looked for him everywhere and scanned the beaches and the ocean. But no sign of Chris. It was speculated that either the currents dragged him out to sea or a shark attacked him. We will never find out. His body was never recovered.

Ruthie was totally devastated. Her life would never be the same. She told me many times: "I lost the love of my life, what am I to do!" Ruthie's eldest daughter who is my second cousin wrote me an e-mail concerning the tragic disappearance of her dad. *"As you wrote, my father's body was never found, and it was very painful for my mother and us, a circle that was very difficult to close, and never did for my mom. I also like to think that finally, they're together."*

I don't think that Ruthie ever did recover from that tragic event. Later in her life, I spent some time with Ruthie at her home in Acapulco. She confided many things to me concerning her love for Chris and what it was like for her to have lost him, seemingly forever. I did everything in my power to console her and tell her that it's never *forever* and that our loved ones are always there waiting for us on the other side. She seemed comforted by my statement.

I was very saddened when I was told she had passed away. She died about 12 years ago, of a massive heart attack. But at the same time, I was happy that she was free and could reunite with Chris, her beloved husband, and soul-mate. Coincidentally, she lived the last 10 years of her life in Acapulco, and her ashes were scattered in Acapulco Bay, just as she wished. I would like to think that she is now with her soul-mate and they continue with their heavenly love affair and nothing can interfere with that everlasting love. Nothing can surpass Love, the brick, and mortar of the Universe in all of its dimensions.

CHAPTER 10

"SORRY, I CAN'T TAKE YOU WITH ME"

"I have not always chosen the safest path. I've made my mistakes, plenty of them. I sometimes jump too soon and fail to appreciate the consequences. But I've learned something important along the way: I've learned to heed the call of my heart. I've learned that the safest path is not always the best path and I've learned that the voice of fear is not always to be trusted."
~Steve Goodier

When I was about ten years old, my parents divorced. My mother said to us: "I can't take you with me back to the States because your father wants to have custody of you. He said he would have four attorneys to my one if I tried to fight it. Besides he will be able to better provide for you." So that was that, and off she went to Los Angeles in an old Buick station wagon loaded with all her earthly possessions. She went to live with my Grandmother and uncle. But before she left, as tears flowed down her cheeks, she cried out: "I will come to visit you as often as I can." My mother was very sentimental. She'd cry instantly and with fluid sadness, especially if it had to do with the drama of life's breakups and lost loves. We were torn up. I thought dreadfully to myself that we were doomed, alone, and with no one to protect us. But I was consoled when too long afterward my stepmother Tere showed up on the scene and became our loving champion and protectress. She was the best thing that could've happened to my messed-up father and to us.

My father sent me off to boarding schools. All of them were Catholic and horrible. I was bullied by the other kids because quite plainly I just didn't fit in. I cried when I was put on the filthy buses to go to these strange failures of institutions so-called schools. But at the same time, I was strangely happy and relieved that I didn't have to put up with the drinking and the abuse. My sisters were safely tucked away at an American nun's school, and they stayed there for years and years. I think they fared much better than their older brother. As I continued to fail at each of the schools that I was put in, the final blow had to come.

No longer knowing what to do with this incorrigible ten-year-old, my grandparents under the strong influence of an extended family member, convinced my father that they had come up with the perfect solution to my problems of mal-assimilation. And that grand plan was to place me in an orphanage run by a foreign priest, whom I will choose to call Father Ignacio. My extended family member was a friend of this priest and spoke to him about me as their *problem*. Fr. Ignacio accepted me into the fold of street urchins, beggars, and abandoned kids. I fit in perfectly because I was also, technically, left behind, first by my mother when she fled to California, and secondly by a binge-drinking father, who at the time, had not the desire or seemingly a concern to raise his son correctly.

In retrospect, it was a blessing. But I traded one abuse for many others. Again, I emphasize this in the context of a soul yearning to learn and not as a defenseless victim yearning to complain and parade my demise, but to learn and to grow.

I felt like I was suddenly thrown under a bridge and told that was your new home. I became depressed and anxious. I would not eat, but even if I wanted to, I couldn't eat the horrible food they served. Most of the time the food was beans, rice, and sometimes soupy, drippy pasta that tasted like overcooked cardboard. There were many compassionate kids who, I don't know if they felt sorry for me or just wanted to help me, but I remember them telling me about the process that I had to follow to eat the pinto beans. I was baffled. "What are you talking about?" I pleaded with alarming disgust. "If you don't scoop out the weevils from the beans, then you eat them, and they'll make you sick," they lied. I became nauseated at the thought and almost threw up. "There are weevils in the beans? What do they look like?" With a roar, they laughed without reproach. But they did teach me how to eat the grub correctly, and I can proudly say that I became an expert at fishing weevils out of the beans. Rarely would we get any meat and if we did it was a small serving. I was not used to the food, and I refused to eat it. When I didn't eat the food, the person in charge of discipline would keep everyone seated at my table until I finished my meal. This sometimes went on for hours at a time, and well into the night when everyone else had gone to bed.

One time, out of frustration, the other kids downed the food when the disciplinarian wasn't looking and then he would release us. But as this happened more and more frequently, the prefect of discipline became suspicious and spied on us. We got caught. He lined us up, and we were instructed to pull down our pants in front of everyone. He took out, what seemed to me at the time, the most massive paddle I had ever seen in my life. The carefully crafted instrument of pain and torture was drilled with some strategically arranged holes to let the air flow with the greatest of ease. He swatted us until our butts were raw. I found myself in another institution of abuse! Today, if this institution were in the United States, there would be outcries and complaints filed before the state child protective agency. Some heads would roll, and licenses would be suspended. But this was rural Mexico. Those protections were nowhere to be found, especially in the 1950's. I'm not sure if Fr. Ignacio was aware of the corporal punishments or not, but I don't have any reason to believe that he didn't know.

If any of the orphans had any family members alive, or who could be located, they were permitted four visiting days a year. The visiting hours lasted from four to six hours. It was strictly prohibited for any orphan to have any family contact whatsoever. One evening as I was forcefully downing the tasteless supper I was served, I looked out through the wire screen that enclosed our makeshift dining room. I saw older people, well-dressed, accompany some helpers who were delivering washing machines, and a large refrigerator. I suddenly recognized my grandparents. I jumped up with joy and with a big smile on my eleven-year-old face ran to the door to go out and give my grandparents a big hug. Suddenly, and without warning, a quick hand grabbed my thin arm and yanked it back. I saw the muscular, dark body of the supervisor, who really was the disciplinarian in chief. He yelled at me saying:

"Where do you think YOU are going?!"

"I'm going to say hello to my grandparents!",

"And who told you could go?"

"But they're my grandparents!"

"Go sit down before I knock you down!"

The kids all started laughing at me. All I could do was to curl up on the hard aluminum bench in front of the cold tables that held the ghastly plastic plates filled with the awful grub they called food, and bury my head in my thin hands and weep and weep and weep. My heart ached to jump into their arms, especially those of my grandmother, but that opportunity was brutally snatched away from me. How could anyone do this to their child? How could a parent abandon their child? These were the thoughts and feelings running through my head. I peered out of my hiding place from time to time to see if they were still there. But, no, they had vanished as quickly as they had appeared. I learned later that these "gifts" were actually my grandparents "payment" for keeping me in that god-awful place. More gifts were delivered at some future date, but at a time when I was conveniently not available. I felt like a prisoner, and I felt abandoned and betrayed. I was angry at my father, my grandparents, and more importantly, my extended family members who had encouraged and campaigned for this ghastly sequestration, convincing my father and grandparents that this was the only hope for me.

BLOODY, BLOODY PANTS

I was frequently told by the kids: "Wait until the day when they tell you that you have to go downtown!" I didn't have a clue what they were talking about. "You won't ever want to pee again, and you're going to walk around as if your legs were attached to sticks and your pants will be all bloody!" The orphans were relentless with these ominous threats, and I was clueless as to their meaning. So, the day came when I was told I had to go downtown. I was terrified.

The orphanage vehicle pulled up to the local Red Cross hospital. The weathered two-story square building appeared to have been built in the early part of the 20th century. Maybe just before the Mexican Revolution of 1910. The central part of the building was open air with a central courtyard and a fountain in the middle. We marched single file through the yard to the waiting area which was filled with sick people coughing and spitting, some holding bloody rags to injuries sustained somewhere, sometime. I walked past blood-stained stretchers. Some were left soaking in the blood-stained water of the decaying fountain. Other pallets were washed down with a hose attached to the courtyard's only water spigot. The rivers of blood from the washed down cots rolled into a single drain, and the workers just carried on as if this was the routine of every day. I thought I was in a war zone where the wounded would have the one and only chance of survival, and from the looks of it, a very dim one at that.

We were all told to be seated on wooden benches in a great walkway with tall ceilings with old paint peeling off the walls. A chilly iodine scented breeze wafted through a barren terrazzo hallway. The younger kids were crying, and the ones who came out were pale and teary with agonizing looks on their faces. Tears rolled down their cheeks, and they yelped in pain as they walked stiffly out of the ward. Some held their blood-stained pants out as to prevent their butchered penises from rubbing against them.

Suddenly a squatty dark-complexioned nurse appeared out of nowhere. Her dark, thick olive skin stood out in high contrast to her bright nurse's white uniform. Her nurse's bonnet sat smartly on her charcoal hair. This was probably the only time in her short life that she held a post of such immense power and control over others. She relished every second of her most important position as she smirked and inspected all of us seated in front of her. She appeared to be quite delighted with her newly starched uniform as she kept checking it for dirt or wrinkles.

"Quien sigue?" "Who's next?" she barked as if she were selling chili peppers at the crowded outdoor market. Everyone pointed at me, and my heart pounded with a frenzy. The Iguana had awakened and was striking in full force with a torrent of adrenaline and cortisol surging through my veins. I could barely walk straight I was so dizzy. I entered a cavernous room with very tall ceilings and with antique light fixtures that had missing light bulbs and those that did have bulbs barely lit the darkened room.

The nurse shouted at me to take my clothes off. "All of them?" "Yes, ALL of them" she screamed in frustration, "How do you think we can operate on you?" "Operate? What are they going to operate on and why? There's nothing wrong with me! Why are they going to operate on me?" I thought to myself as tears streamed down my cheeks. I shyly turned away from the nurse and pulled down my shorts. I covered my privates with my eleven-year-old hands. She laughed as did the other nurses. Two nurses hauled me onto the operating table my hands still covering myself. "Quita las manos güerito!" "Take your hands away little blondie!" There was a huge, 1930's spotlight that precariously hung over the decaying operating table. It looked like it might have been imported from England as war surplus spotlighting incoming Nazi bombers in the London blitz. If I didn't get killed by Dr. Enchilada, the overhanging spotlight would do the trick just as well, and there might not be anything left to cut! No doctor needed! Poof! Done! Gone!

I reluctantly removed my hands, and the almighty nurse took a swab of cotton and painted my groin and prepubescent privates in iodine orange with almost stabbing strokes. It must've been the new orange of groin fashion. "I'm glad we don't have to shave you, that just takes too much of our time, and then your older pals get too excited, and we have to slap it down!" she gravely announced to her snickering indigenous turned-suddenly-nurse audience. I couldn't believe what was coming out of her big mouth. Her crooked teeth were a lovely shade of tobacco stained yellow. How glamorous! The words came spilling out of her thick lips smeared in the reddest of lipsticks, and her smoke tainted breath could've gassed a burro. She could've fought a bull with her voluptuous lava red lips, no cape needed!

Suddenly, she yelled over to the doctor: "Mire doctor, yo creo que este güerito ya está!" "Look, doctor, I think this little white boy here is all fixed." He snapped back at her and said: "You don't say 'fixed,' he's circumcised." "Si por supuesto doctor," "Yes, of course, doctor," she humbly mumbled her way into chastisement. He reluctantly ambled over to the old operating table without ever establishing eye contact with the puny, skinny, defenseless, and naked eleven-year-old boy. He gave it a quick look over and barked at the nurse: "Get him down!" Immediately the nurse told me sarcastically: "Te salvaste güerito!" "You got saved, little white boy!"

I jumped off the table as if it was on fire, no one helped me this time, and I furiously pulled on my shorts over my freshly painted orange groin. I was so anxious to get out of there that I slipped my pants on backward. The red-mouthed nurse laughed as if she'd just got fondled by the local banana peddler in the middle of the open-air market. I corrected my pants error and flew out of that room as fast as I could. She followed right behind me, and I thought for a second she had changed her mind, and she was going to haul me back onto the butcher's table. I was relieved when she re-issued her barking orders to the other kids sitting on the bench. The kids in the waiting area couldn't believe that I was done so fast and that I wasn't crying or holding my groin. They weren't too happy with me, either. Everyone had to be circumcised whether they wanted it or not, needed it or not, or had an infection or not. If I recall correctly, some of the town doctors had volunteered to circumcise the orphans because they felt that they were making a real contribution to the health of the children. This was so because a few of them had indeed developed infections. I never recalled participating in any talks on hygiene, especially if it had to do with the male reproductive organ. That was strictly taboo, you just didn't talk about sex in those days.

I personally believe that circumcision is a delicate decision that parents have to make on their own and I respect their choices. However, I wished that I could've made that decision for myself because it is my body and my choosing, and mine only to make. In this case, I'm grateful I had already been circumcised but apparently not for the same reasons.

I have always disagreed with the U.S. medical field which encouraged and propagated the practice of circumcision. I wish my parents had not taken from me the power to make my own choices about my own body. Recently, I read the American Academy of Pediatrics' official policy on circumcision, and I found it to harmonize with my beliefs and feelings:

"Existing scientific evidence demonstrates potential medical benefits of newborn male circumcision; however, these data are not sufficient to recommend routine neonatal circumcision. In circumstances, there are potential benefits and risks, yet the procedure is not essential to the child's current well-being, parents should determine what is in the best interest of the child."

CHAPTER 11

THE SEMINARY

"It is customary to blame secular science and anti-religious philosophy for the eclipse of religion in modern society. It would be more honest to blame religion for its own defeats. Religion declined not because it was refuted, but because it became irrelevant, dull, oppressive, insipid. When faith is completely replaced by creed, worship by discipline, love by habit; when the crisis of today is ignored because of the splendor of the past; when faith becomes an heirloom rather than a living fountain; when religion speaks only in the name of authority rather than with the voice of compassion—its message becomes meaningless."
~ Rabbi Abraham Joshua Heschel
(God in Search of Man: A Philosophy of Judaism)

After a couple of years, I plotted to make my escape from the orphanage. I decided that I suddenly *developed* a vocation to become a priest. In Latin America, they took seminarians at a very young age; I was eleven and ripe for the picking.......in more ways than one. So, I announced to Fr. Ignacio that I was interested in entering the local seminary and requested his permission to go to the monthly orientation meetings downtown at the 16th-century church. He grilled me about this *sudden vocation* of mine. I convinced him that I did, indeed, felt this calling from the *Lord*, but I wanted to have an opportunity to check it out for myself. He reluctantly gave me permission to leave the high walled compound. No one was permitted to go anywhere for any reason other than for an infrequent necessity. Today this confined compound reminds me of the precious value of freedom. The only way to get out of the place was either on a field trip or an escorted trip to a dentist, doctor's office, or the penis chopping block at the World War II hospital, which ironically, was right across the street from the main church. When I did leave to go downtown to the church, I would have to take the old rickety town buses. But fortunately, I was able to go downtown unescorted. I had no idea why that exception was made for me, but my gratefulness knew no bounds.

The bus route passed by my grandparents' house. As the bus bounced by the enormous backyard of their house, I would stretch my skinny neck as far as it could reach up over the seat to see if I could spot, at least the gardener or if I was lucky one of my grandparents. Every time I passed the house, no one was in sight. My disappointment gripped my throat and nudged a tear or two from my eyes. One day as I made my way back from the orientation sessions and the bus neared my grandparents' home, I got up enough courage to suddenly pull the bus stop cord, high above my seat.

I quickly exited the old beat-up bus and ran to the street where my grandparent's house was patiently waiting for me. I decided that I would surprise them with my unexpected visit. They were ecstatic to see me. My grandmother screamed with delight and almost cried when she saw me. I never knew if Mamanita cried of happiness or sorrow, to see how thin and emaciated I had become. Perhaps it was both. Upon reflection, I'm sure of it.

Mamanita ordered our cook, Angela, to fix me a steak dinner. Angela was thrilled to see me as well. We grew up with her, and we considered her a part of the family. That was the treat of all treats! I gobbled down the food as fast as I could and with such desperation as if someone was going to steal it from me. I savored every bite, and as I did, anger welled up at the thought of how insipid the food was at the orphanage. I deserved better. My rage was also directed at that particular extended family member who had convinced my father and my grandfather that Father Ignacio's outfit was the best option for me. My grandmother told my father and grandfather that enough was enough. I should just stay at home with them and not go back to the orphanage. But they firmly rejected that option. I had my own life there, and eventually, I would leave for the seminary. I wanted to stay there with them, but I knew that I had to go back or face trouble. I departed my grandparent's house with tears in my eyes, As I slowly walked back to the main boulevard, eyes cast downward, the thought of leaving the orphanage, suddenly cheered me up. I took the next bus back to the orphanage. But my tummy was full, and my heart was contented to have had the chance to enjoy my grandparents. Unbelievably even my father, who was uncharacteristically sober at 6 pm in the afternoon, was cordial and welcoming.

As for Fr. Ignacio, the 11-year-old me was not fond of him. I saw him more as my captor, benevolent as he may have been. Today, the adult me admires him significantly, and I recognize the work of love that he undertook in helping thousands of orphaned children. His work continues today, even after years of his passing. I hold reflective respect for his profound spirituality, and in part, I attribute the development of my own spirituality in light of his love and generous spirit. Spirit saw to it that I had contact with this spiritual giant, for reasons that I do not know. Fr. Ignacio was, in my opinion, an example of what all of those who claim to be ministers or priests could be doing, by following his example. Fr. Ignacio walked his truth without riches or benefits. He practiced what he preached.

The truth is that Love is all that matters. Love conquers all. I believe Fr. Ignacio is a saint, and the Catholic church will eventually formalize that fact, even though, in my opinion, it is not necessary for any human organization to adulate the enormous work he or any other person performed for mankind. His work stands on its own merits as a witness to the magnificence of his soul. The pure unconditional love that flows through him and which we all share as part of our own spark of divinity is evidenced today by his works. We are all connected and interconnected in a cloth of seamless weavings of divine love and wisdom. To deny that is to deny our very own existence as manifestations of Spirit or the One Which Is All That Is or the Ground of All Being. The following brief quote from Senator Cory Booker summarizes that unconditional love: *"Don't speak to me about your religion; first, show it to me in how you treat other people. Don't tell me how much you love your God; show me in how much you love all God's children."*

I finally agreed to apply for admission to the seminary, and I was accepted. I announced my approved entry to Fr. Ignacio, and he spoke to my father and grandparents. Once it had been agreed that I could go off to the seminary, Fr. Ignacio said to me: "You know Patrick you are making a significant decision and I support you. However, you must know that once you leave our institution, you cannot come back to us ever again." "Yes, I know Father, but my vocation is pretty clear to me." I silently giggled to myself. To think that I would be devastated to be banished forever from that place seemed so comedic to me at the time. However, now I do appreciate how I grew and learned from that experience.

It appeared that my father was not too keen on the matter......his son a priest? There is something wrong here. But he reluctantly agreed to let me go, probably suspecting that it was a passing whim and I would tire of that venture as well. If that's what he was thinking, he was right. The tuition was minimal, and I was very eager to get out of the orphanage. I was free!

The seminary was a new challenge. My new-found freedom was not really freedom at all. I suddenly realized that I had jumped from the frying pan right into the fire. I was restricted by schedules, prayers, masses, rituals, and more rules than the Vatican's book of Canon Law. Quite frankly, I wasn't quite ready for rubrics, and I undoubtedly was not prepared for all the dogma. But I was looking forward to a better environment and by far the most delicious food I had tasted in a very long time.

IGUANAS ARE CATHOLIC?

This point in my life, formalized the beginning of indoctrination of many toxic concepts as taught by organized religion, in this case, the Catholic Church. Those poisonous beliefs included, hell, purgatory, devil, satan, (I refuse to capitalize a name of something that does not exist) sinner, sins, unworthiness, and the list went on and on. Being as young as I was, it did not work in my favor. Youth tend to be very susceptible to indoctrination and for the most part that instruction is fear based, primarily when referring to the existence of devils, demons, satan, etc., More on this later.

One of the hallmarks of toxic belief systems, aside from promoting reptilian thinking and behaviors, is that they tend to be exclusive as opposed to being inclusive. By that it was meant that certain groups of people whose life conditions were one way or another would be excluded from participating in the rites of the Catholic Church. For example, if you weren't Catholic you were automatically banned from the sacraments, or worse, banned from *Heaven*. That was a presumptuous and pompous edict to impose on human beings. That may have changed today. However, I think it's a bit too late for those of us who were fed that basket of lies. We were led to believe that divorce was a sin. Therefore, one was also banned from the sacraments (exclusiveness). Women can never be ordained as priests and serve the members of the Church. Women are not entitled to that privilege, only men (exclusiveness). The masculine elements in any organization have to be balanced and be complemented by the feminine aspects of the same system. It's the natural Yin and Yang so nobly taught by Lao-Tzu 2540 years ago. Niels Bohr, the great physicist, created his coat of arms around the Tai-Chi symbol of Yin and Yang.

Dr. Bohr recognized that the laws of physics reflect the dynamic interplay of opposites within the unified field of all possibilities. He designed his coat of arms in the traditional representation of the principle of complementarity on which he based his views of the fundamental laws of physics. Also known as the wave-particle duality, this principle stresses that physical fields have properties which are usually attributed *either* to particles *or* to waves. If physicists recognize the laws of complementarity, the Church appears to be wholly uncomplimentary and oblivious to it in theory or practice.

Initially, I began writing about these subjects, and I felt my tone was somewhat attacking and negativistic, understandably so, considering my experiences and the impacts they had on my person. So, I asked myself the question: How would Jesus, or Buddha, or Lao-Tzu or Mohammed approach these same subjects?

I contemplated what set these masters apart from mankind in general. What sprung to my heart was the Divine Essence these Masters radiated, which is pure Unconditional Love. I would like to think that they would have probably asked open-ended questions to address them. For example: Assuming that the leaders of the church, from the Pope on down to the parish priests or deacons, were willing to set aside their prejudices, and shift old-worn out paradigms to the inclusiveness-based paradigms these Masters emulated, what would the impacts these changes in thinking might have upon mankind?

The open-ended questions might look something like these:

1. What would happen if we declare that all people, regardless of their, race, socioeconomic status and sexual orientation be welcomed to participate in all of our churches? (including enjoying the right to be married in the church). How might this impact this population positively or negatively?
2. How might these same populations feel and act if we invited them to be leaders in their own right and even be welcomed into the ministry of their choosing?
3. We can readily recognize that sex is a natural and healthy function of the human body. Can we debate that sexual desires conform to God's plan for mankind without imparting judgments on it

(making it a sin)? Can we recognize that sex is one of the most beautiful and powerful forces in nature? What might happen if we permitted our clergy to marry and still be able to carry on their pastoral duties, like their Protestant colleagues?

4. What might happen if the Church no longer passed judgment on what the clergy considers people's *sinful and immoral behaviors?* How would congregants be impacted? How might their attitudes change or not change? Might they accept sexuality as part of God's creation and not as an aberrant bodily function to hate and repress?

5. If we were willing to permit these changes might we be able to increase our overall membership and participation so that the faithful would be more inclined to follow the Master's teachings of unconditional love?

6. How would it impact divorced couples if they are entirely accepted back into the church be allowed to participate in all its activities and rituals?

7. How would divorce coupled be impacted if allowed to remarry in the church if they so desired?

8. How would allowing women to be priests contribute to the health and well-being of their congregations?

9. How might people feel and act by eliminating all of the fear-based doctrines and dogma the churches preach? And these are replaced with positive and inspirational ideas? Would people live a more stress-free life? Might they be more productive in their lives as a result? Might it give them hope for a beautiful afterlife devoid of fear and the invented concepts of hell and damnation?

I suspect that those in the church or those who are closely affiliated with it might have some angry reactions to these questions. Undoubtedly, the ego would play a significant role in fostering negative replies. Or Paradigm Paralysis may prevent church officials from making positive changes because of their recalcitrance to throw out their old paradigms. (more on Paradigms later). However, if we as humans, take the same stand as did the Master, that Love is All There Is and is the sum total of the law and the prophets, then we would look more benevolently upon our brothers and sisters and compassionately welcome them back into the fold.

Again, the critical question is the following: *What would the Master do?* Knowing that He is the embodiment of pure Unconditional Love, I think we all know, deep down in our hearts, that he would extend his arms to all people and welcome them into the fold with His full embrace. All ego aside, we do know that! And, deep down we know that we know that!

CHAPTER 12

THE DUNGEON OF BONES
AND A DEAD CHILD?

*"Life and death are one thread, the same
line viewed from different sides."*
~Lao Tzu

So, I did not fare well in my first year in the seminary. Weekly, I would get written up by the Prefect of Discipline for one violation or another. Instinctively I rebelled against the doctrines, the rules, the do's and the don'ts. I frequently violated one regulation or another, getting in trouble over one thing or another. One of those violations included an unauthorized trip to the vast underground Cathedral's crypt.

One day, a group of us were talking to one of the older seminarians. He told us that there was a crypt underneath the church.

I innocently asked: "What's a crypt?" They all roared with laughter.

"You mean you don't know what a crypt is?" "Where did you grow up?" I felt embarrassed by my ignorance.

"It's where the dead were buried many centuries ago, including not too long ago. Their bones are still down there."

"No! That's a lie, it can't be! That's why we have cemeteries," I responded with a faked sense of knowing.

"Well, we don't have to argue about it, let's go down there and find out for ourselves."

"But we aren't allowed to go there," protested another of the more rule-abiding seminarians, "They're digging up the bones and going to turn it into a usable crypt."

"So, if we are to go, we better get down there before they remove all the bones!" I thought he was joking, but I saw that he was dead serious (pun intended!).

He continued: "We need to go at the right time when the Prefect and the other priests are meeting with the Archbishop. I think then we can go without getting caught."

So, we timed the perfect adventure at the precise time when we supposedly would not get caught.

It was about 4 pm, and we sneaked into the sacristy of the Cathedral. Two ancient wooden doors, stood menacingly in front of us almost as if warning us not to trespass. The iron-studded doors were heavy, and it took two of the more muscular seminarians to pry one of the doors open. As it swung open, the unoiled hinges creaked eerily that seemed to send out a second warning not to enter the subterranean cemetery. My heart beat faster. Everyone was given a candle, and a few of my colleagues carried flashlights. I assumed the candles were to be lit to say some prayers for the dead or something like that.

"Turn on the lights" I yelled as we started to descend the steep stoned-laid stairs, ancient with morbid history. Laughter broke out.

"Do you think there would be electricity down here?" "Why do you think we brought candles dummy."

In that instant, someone lit a candle and passed it around, so everyone lit their torch to guide them.

The air was stagnant and exceptionally damp. It reeked of mustiness and the forbidding odor of death. The breeze blown flames from the candles threw menacing shadows upon the humid water-stained walls. Runoff from the rain above filtered through the ancient foundations and the walls were stained with streaked calcium deposits. They appeared as a ghost silently observing our every move. We reached the bottom of the steep stone masonry stairs where we landed on dirt. In front of me was a huge stone pillar that was 8 feet long by 6 feet wide.

"What's that?" I enquired sheepishly for fear of being laughed at again.

"That's the bottom of the main altar," one of the more knowledgeable of the seminarians cried out. According to Canon Law, the base of the main altar of a cathedral had to sit firmly on the soil where the church was built. But I really could've cared less. I was too preoccupied with what lay beyond the stone pillar.

The Archbishop at the time completely renovated the church. Many other leaders in the Catholic church at that time were similarly embroiled in the denuding of the *distractions* of statuary and other interruptions of the Mass and the homilies. He stripped it of the 16th-century statues and altars and converted it into a *modern* church. He proclaimed that the faithful should not be distracted by statues and other religious objects and should be paying attention to the Mass and his, or the celebrant's homily. But the people weren't happy with him. They accused him of being a communist and stirring up trouble. Liberation Theology is what they called it at the time. He was a controversial cleric.

He did away with all the statues except two that I remember. My father was not much of a churchgoer, but before I went to the orphanage and the seminary, he insisted we attend Mass on Sundays, while at the same time he smoked cigarettes in the church's courtyard. When we went down to the main church, he paid devout reverence to the statue of St. Christopher. He said that St. Christopher saved him and my mother in a horrible car wreck shortly after they were married in the 1940's. He attributed the survival to a medal of St. Christopher that he had attached to the coup's sunshade. My father was devastated and profoundly disappointed when the church removed St. Christopher's feast day in favor of more modern and *relevant* Saints. He said to me that they didn't know what they were talking about and nobody was going to take his St. Christopher away from him. I had to acknowledge him for taking a stand like that. In a way, I was surprisingly proud of him.

We walked further into the dark bowels of the crypt. We struggled to keep our candles burning as the drafty cavern menacingly plotted to blow them out. Some had to relight theirs with much difficulty. As we turned a very dark and ominous corner, I was stunned by what I saw. Unsuspecting of what my eyes were gazing upon, a pile of all sorts of human bones at least 6 feet tall, suddenly emerged out of the darkness of the dungeon bathed in the faint glare of the dancing candle lights. I gasped! – "How could this be?!" I thought to myself. When I turned my head and saw an assortment of old coffins. I held my breath filling my lungs with the stench of the stagnant odor of death that hung like a cloud throughout this cold den of mortality. As I continued walking by the dim light of the flickering flame of my now almost consumed candle, my eyesight fell upon the small, partially opened coffin of what appeared to be of an infant child. I could see a small dress that blanketed the shrinking little corpse. I suddenly turned my sight away, but it was too late as the deep morbid impression left a deep etch on my consciousness.

My heart was pounding even harder, and I yelled out in a panic: "I need to get out of here!!" My lament was met with mocking laughter.

"He's scared! Let's open one of the coffins!" they derisively chanted.

I turned to run out and then.................everything went black. I lost consciousness.

I awoke dangling on a beam, my arms, and feet hanging over a dark empty pit. "Where am I?" I screamed at the top of my voice. I heard a voice high above the darkness: "I told you we shouldn't have brought him down here!"

"Quiet, someone is going to hear us!!" I then felt a hand grab my pants belt and lift my 75 pounds or so, up, out of a dark hole. "What did I fall into?" I asked disoriented with tears streaming down my cheeks. "I think you were in a pit that was being dug to bury the bones and you were caught by a cross beam." My Guardian Angels must've really been working overtime that day because I didn't fall to the bottom of the pit.

We hurried out of the dark and foreboding bowels of the church. I was bruised, cut, and bleeding down my face and my shirt was covered in blood. I was so relieved to have survived that literal descent into hell. The older seminarians took me to the infirmary to clean me up and bandage my wounds. We thought of an original story to tell that wouldn't raise suspicion. The rector didn't question the supposed fall that I had suffered in "one of the corridors of the building." We didn't get caught, and we never spoke about that adventure ever again, especially me. I had nightmares of hanging on the beam and skeleton hands reaching up to grab my small frame body to throw me into the pit of death from whence they came. Those nightmares lasted far too long afterward.

This incident is what I would call today fresh food for the iguana. Keep the amygdala fed and trained, and it will be conditioned for life. It has been discussed by many psychologists and psychiatrists that a well-trained reptilian brain only perfects its original design to permit our survival. The problem with my amygdala is that it was very well trained and got better and better at sounding the alarms, bells, and whistles. The iguana was always on edge and ready to strike.

One of the most significant privileges during the first year at the seminary was to be vested with your cassock. It was black with a white sash. It was quite the honor. I was denied the cassock the first year because of my unruliness. I was devastated. I had to endure the embarrassment of wearing civilian clothes with the other misfits. However, after another year of better conduct and increasing maturity (puberty arrived just in time), I was finally bestowed the cherished cassock and sash. I lasted only 2 years in the seminary. I didn't fit in there, and the dogma, the rituals, the do's and don'ts that are so common in an institution of religion, became very tedious, indeed.

This was one of the first lessons in my life that taught me that things weren't what they first appeared to be. I believed that entering the seminary would help me become more *spiritual* without really knowing what that meant. My expectations included being surrounded by holy men in search of a mission to accomplish, a task that involved helping others. But that's not what I found. I found boys, adolescents, and men who were just like everyone else who didn't have a clue what life was all about and much less about spirituality, though they went through all the routines and rituals. I don't know what I expected, but I didn't get all my expectations met. I was disappointed.

I found the same competition for power and position that I saw in the orphanage among both the staff and the seminarians. Nevertheless, the seminary was an essential first lesson about the hypocrisy of the less spiritual of our church institutions. It was my first lesson in the hypnotic process of religious and social conditioning and indoctrination. Bend their minds to do this, and they will succumb to do the other. Have them always under your mental power and control. But still, have them believe that they have the upper hand when in reality they don't. Preach fear and lies to the people, and you will be able to control them till they die. At least, that was the practice, and the consequences we see today are increasingly empty churches and fewer and fewer priests to minister to the people.

WAS THE INFANT DEAD?

An excellent example of this, one day, I was in charge of being the door attendant of the seminary. We were given monthly assignments on a rotating basis, and this was one of them. The bell rang, and I went to open the heavy wooden hacienda type steel reinforced door. As I did so, a short indigenous woman appeared wrapped with a gray and black rebozo (peasant shawl) over her head. The woman carried her baby in a sling formed from her cloak. The woman's face was covered in tears, and she said,

"Please Padre, my child just died, and he hasn't been baptized could you please baptize him. I don't want him to go to Purgatory or Hell, that's the last thing I want for my child."

Alarmed and with a quickening sense of urgency I told her:

"I'm not a priest Señora, but I will get one for you, please come in and sit down."

She brushed her tears away with her one free wrinkled hand and delicately cradling her bundle of flesh and bones, sat on the cold cement bench in the reception room.

I hurriedly combed the seminary in search of a priest. I was told that they were all in a meeting with the Archbishop. They were always meeting with the damn Archbishop, I fumed to myself. So, I returned empty-handed with no priest in tow and explained my dilemma to the petite, grief-stricken woman who was rocking and hugging the small bundle that she held close to her chest.

"But you can baptize him" she pleaded wiping her tear-drenched face.

"You are wearing a cassock, so that gives you the power to save my child so he won't go to Purgatory," I remembered, and I might add correctly, that according to Canon Law, in the absence of a cleric and in a case of absolute emergency, any layperson could baptize.

Without thinking further, and to bring solace and comfort to an unfortunate grieving woman, I went for a glass of water and uncovered the listless baby's head.

"I baptize you in the name of the Father, and the Son and the Holy Spirit."

The woman hurriedly blessed herself with the sign of the cross and returned to her tears and thanked me endlessly. Between sobs, she took my hand and attempted to kiss it, but I objected and held my hand firmly by my side, but her insistence on kissing my hand won out. She kept repeating over and over again: "Now he is saved, gracias, muchas gracias padre!"

She left immediately as if hurrying to find a burial place for the child. Without turning back her gaze at me, she clutched her little bundle tightly covered in freshly shed droplets of grief and sadness. All I could do was just stop and stare at her. I was not prepared for what happened. Was the child dead? I will never know. Was she just doing that for attention? Or was the baby really dead and she sought relief knowing that her child would now be going to heaven instead of Purgatory?

To this day, I don't know the answer to any of these questions. However, can I say that I made a difference in that woman's life? Did I inspire a breath of hope for that woman? Very possibly. I know not the answer to those questions either. Was it earth-shattering? I hardly can claim that. But I did feel right about comforting a desperately destitute woman.

Today, as I remember that event, I feel a deep connection to that woman and especially to the child. I established a bridge of loving care for a little human being, innocent and helpless, whether dead or alive. The joy that I felt, knowing that I had impacted another human's life, even at my tender age of 13, enlarges my heart and comforts my soul, even to this day. I was very proud of my act of compassion. I felt good about myself.

So, I had to let my superiors know what had transpired. When I told them, they just laughed at me and shook their heads and gave me their stupid-little-kid look. My feelings were hurt, but I believed at that time, as did that woman, that something miraculous happened in those 10 seconds as the water streamed down the tiny baby's cold head. In both the woman's mind and my own (at that time), the trickle of holy water liberated that child's soul. That was huge for me as I believed it was for the mother and her tiny infant in that sacred moment of baptism. That event which took place somewhere in time and space was our very own truth and source of comfort. It was our very own truth that no man could interfere with, not even my self-centered and cold superiors.

As I look back and contemplate that moment, my beliefs have changed drastically about Purgatory and Hell and all that nonsense. However, what I believe has survived from that incident, in both the peasant woman's heart and mine, is the act of caring for someone unknown in a moment of real desperation. A 13-year-old and a peasant woman with an infant, possibly dead, how often does that happen?

I reflected on my superior's attitude. I learned that even though the cleric mocked my generosity of heart, I knew that I did the right thing, for my sake and that of the indigenous woman and her child. What would've been the impact on me had those priests said: "You did an outstanding deed Patrick, we admire you for helping that woman today?" I probably would've learned that paying a compliment is far more dignified and validating than mockery. Only the beautiful display of love survived and that is all that will ever survive because unconditional love is the construct of the Universe and the very essence of Source – or All That Is.

I knew that I wasn't going to be staying very long at the seminary. This final incident left a deep wound in my psyche. I knew at that point that I was headed for the same destiny of those who no longer could live in such a sterile environment. It happened that those seminarians who were either kicked out or who left on their own accord would secretly disappear, literally, from one day to the next. We would suddenly find their belongings packed up, their lockers empty, and no one dared to even ask what happened to them. If you asked, you were immediately disciplined and admonished. It was literally like the KGB or the Gestapo abducted them in the middle of the night, for we never witnessed their disappearance. There were no "good-byes," no "I wish you the best in the future." Nothing so humane as that. How strangely bizarre this all seemed to me.

CHAPTER 13

CHANGE: THE ONLY CONSTANT
IN THE UNIVERSE

*"Change is the law of life. And those who look only to
the past or present are certain to miss the future."*
~ John F. Kennedy

*"Faith is not the clinging to a shrine but
an endless pilgrimage of the heart."*
~ Rabbi Abraham Joshua Heschel

As if the 50's didn't bring enough cultural surprises, the early 60's prepped us to anticipate a long awaited-freedom from the closed and narrow-mindedness of the previous decades. Some organizations are flexible, and they advance in rhythm with changing times. But for some institutions, paradigm paralysis is firmly entrenched and is utterly unyielding. In the Summer of 1961, much to my surprise, the seminary vacated the 16th-century monastery of the big city and moved all of its population to a secluded little pueblo where a more ancient church and adjacent early sixteenth-century monastery was waiting with open arms for all the *Padres to be*. The move was only for June and July.

Electricity had yet to discover the sleepy little town. The seminary Rector acquired an old, noisy World War II American generator that served to dimly and sparsely light the eerie arched hallways and corridors of the ancient Augustinian cloister. Electric wires hung precariously from pillar to pillar nailed into the stucco wall. The generator hours of operation, if I recall correctly, were from sundown to, literally "lights out" at 10 pm. After that, it was a flashlight or candle or both.

We lighted our way with candles many nights when the generator went on strike. Walking through the corridors of those ancient shadowy and breezy hallways were the eeriest experiences of my life, not unlike the descent into the Cathedral's crypt and its seemingly bottomless pit. I got caught many a night alone for some odd reason or another, and I couldn't walk fast enough to catch up with some other human that could break the spell in my brain that the monks of old were diligently following me and my footsteps.

The Iguana loved those nights and was on full alert to help me imagine the hooded Spanish monks of yesteryear spying on my nightly strolls waiting to strike at me and pull me into another hole in a crypt full of ancient bones. I had bizarre and familiar sensations, like remembering times gone past when all we had for lighting were candles or oil lamps. It felt oddly part of my being, and I felt surprisingly comfortable with the luminesce of the waxy torches that cast their golden glows upon the thick walls of the friary. Were these vague memories of past lives living in monasteries as a monk, or priest or a nun? Who knows. But like the Church of old, I firmly know that Reincarnation is real. I find candles most alluring with almost a romantic flair. Their soft glare romantically seduces the darkness into a cozy and pleasant warmness!

Our beds were old steel framed single beds with flimsy mattresses sprinkled with an abundance of bloodthirsty bed bugs. We had to methodically pump DDT (in the 60's that's all we had as an insecticide) into every crevice of the beds. The almost flat mattresses that were doled out to us also had to be treated for the pests. There was so much DDT flying around in the long high domed chambers that had been converted into dormitories, that it looked and smelled like an insecticide factory. A crop duster couldn't have done any better. It's a wonder we didn't get sick from the exposure.

We were blessed to have a beautiful orchard attached to the side of the monastery that was filled with a rich assortment of juicy oranges, guavas, apples, plums, and other fruits. We could pick the fruits of our choice at any time we wished. We were also fortunate to have, as we did in the city monastery, a group of charming and well-educated community of nuns who served us tasty meals. Water at the site was a problem, as it was generally in all of Mexico. To drink from the tap was to sentence your intestines to eternal damnation and the painful curse of a thousand Aztec warriors battling for the last morsel of food for conversion to runny mush, and dispel it at its own displeasure at the most inconvenient time and place possible. And whatever food was in the stomach was destined to erupt more violently than the worse eruption of the nearby fuming volcanoes.

The nuns who cooked the meals were also charged with purifying the water in the most ancient but effective way I have ever seen to this day in Mexico or elsewhere. They relied on a massive volcanic rock, cradled precariously on a reinforced wooden stand. The volcanic filter appeared porous from eons of past gaseous bubbles of sulfuric gases released during the many eruptions of the fiery mountain's long history. The top portion of the rock contained a sizeable basin-like cavity in which the water from the monastery's old well was poured. As the water slowly seeped through the porous rock, it dripped in large colorful and finely decorated clay pots where the purified water accumulated drops at a time. That was the source of our drinking water and never did I recall ever getting sick from drinking it. The sisters cooked delicious and varied meals. They also made the tastiest guava preserves or sweet paste called "guayabate." To this day I have never tasted a desert so fruity, fresh and flavorful as guayabate.

For entertainment at our "summer retreat" there were soccer matches, hikes, outings, or board games that we had available to play. Another form of creepy entertainment was sitting around and listening to one of our classmates read the published stories and spooky ghost legends of the little pueblo where we were vacationing. The tales of hauntings and crazy monks crying in the corridors of the monastery we were living in, gave the iguana some good food to munch on!

But our time was not solely occupied in play. We had to keep brushing up on our Latin (which I hated with an absolute passion) and being behind in my studies required extra attention supplied by able tutors, mainly, older seminarians who were assigned to me. I disdained the chore as much as they did. Working with me was a task in itself. Who cares about a language that only was spoken by the Catholic church and even then, it was on its way out thanks to the Second Vatican Council.

The other form of entertainment involved me, of all people. The rector had an old 16 mm projector and was very anxious to use it. Fr. Roberto loved to show off how he had become suddenly modern and, thus, so significant in the eyes of his charges. He wanted to show movies to the seminarians and enrich them with a little foreign culture. One day he asked me if my father knew who might have some films that we could show to the seminarians. I told him that I didn't think my father could help us with that, but I said that the Benjamin Franklin Library in Mexico City had a whole catalog of exciting films and documentaries.

The library was part of the American Embassy and at that time was under the U.S. Information Service (USIS). So, he diligently assigned an older seminarian to take me on a long bus trip south to Mexico City and we brought back several films that I thought might be a hit. One of those was about a group of Soviet Ballet dancers that were performing in the United States and how they devised a plot to defect from the evil Soviet Union to the freedom-loving United States of America. It was American propaganda, at its Cold War finest. The screen filled with ballerinas frantically dancing in their tights tutus, feathers flying in all directions. Their uncovered shoulders and bare long and trim legs made Fr. Roberto cringe at every pirouette, which required he immediately placed cardboard in front of the lens of the projector. The carton flew back and forth in front of the projector's lenses, faster than a swinging pendulum of an ancient clock. Finally, and with no warning, he angrily shut off the projector and said: "the show's over!" His hand and arm must have just given out, and he must've said to himself *the hell with this*. The seminarians voiced their disapproval but were quickly rebuked for their insolence.

They weren't the only ones rebuked. I was firmly admonished for my excellent selection of material that was considered as *obscene*. Go figure! That type of film could never be shown to a group of virtuous seminarians who are "to serve the Lord in chastity and obedience."

That was the last trip to the Benjamin Library. I told him that the library had nothing exciting to watch. And that was the end of the projector and the "Super-Duper Summer Film Festival of the Summer Seminary of 1961!" The same old, rancid, mentality and deplorable paralysis of the Catholic hierarchy was alive and well. Quite frankly, as I look back at it, I can still say, that nothing much seems to have changed.

CHAPTER 14

FREEDOM TO A NEW LAND

"Give me your tired, your poor, your huddled masses yearning to breathe free."
~ Emma Lazarus

Finally, the day came that I left the seminary. As expected, I was given *secret* instructions to pack all of my belongings at a specific time when all the other seminarians were unavailable to witness my exit. I was then swiftly escorted to the same doors where I baptized the infant child cuddled in her sad mother's arms. The event came flashing into my awareness like a lightning bolt, including the harassment of my superiors. Once I stepped out of the massive wooden doors that separated centuries of old worn-out thinking from the reality of the real world, it ignited in me utter joy and happiness to finally be free from that sterile environment. I almost wanted to jump for joy that I didn't have to deal with that stagnated centuries-old mindset.

Once I was home, I was free to come and go as I pleased. The first emotions for me as I explored my new-found freedom was an absolute joy, like the first time I learned to walk. Oh! I could go here, and I could go there! And I didn't have to ask the superior for permission! But then again, being back home, meant that I had to possibly face the wearisome alcoholism of my father. But for some reason, things seemed tame in comparison to previous years. There was a certain détente operating almost by *divine decree*. That made my life tolerable for a change, but of course, it wasn't entirely devoid of unpleasant incidents.

There was a renewed conversation taking place between my father and my grandfather as to the next step to deal with the problem of Patrick McKallick. Maybe they didn't quite put it that way, but that's what it felt like to me. However, their solution was, without a doubt, very appealing to me. My grandfather had been talking with his acquaintances about schools in the U.S. where they could send me. My English was not spectacular, as a matter of fact, it was disastrous. I spoke with a Spanish accent, and English grammar was an unknown that I eventually would have to master.

But above all, according to my grandfather, I needed to get a good American education. I am forever indebted to him for encouraging this, and I believe, in part, to have funded my Jr. and Sr. High School. So, they picked out a Catholic boarding school that had an excellent ESL (English as Second Language) program. It was in Arkansas, (of all places!) in a small town 50 miles Northeast of Little Rock as the crow flies. The school was way out in the woods some 9 miles west of the rural village. It was run by the Third Order of the Brothers of Saint Francis of the Poor.

I flew to San Antonio from Mexico City with my father. Since I was a little boy, I loved everything that had wings and could fly. We flew up on an American Airlines DC-6, and that was so exciting! I enjoyed every moment of it. Our stop-over in San Antonio was necessary for some shopping. We went downtown to the J.C. Penney's on Houston St. and Joske's Department store. There were no shopping malls back in the early 60's, at least not in San Antonio. My father was exceptionally generous, and he did treat me to some decent clothes and shoes, and everything that a 14-year-old would need for boarding school.

Everything was so different than Mexico. The streets were clean, and the people were so polite. I hardly heard any honking of horns, and I thought that was so out of the norm compared to what I was used to from the chaos of Mexico, especially Mexico City. The city buses were air-conditioned! I couldn't believe it! The food was different as well. I quickly grew very accustomed to cheeseburgers with fries, and chocolate milkshakes. That was heaven! I was especially grateful to my father for being so pleasant and in such a good mood. More importantly, he was well behaved on this trip without any drunken episodes or drama. We visited my many aunts and uncles and other relatives who lived in San Antonio and established new relationships with relatives that were previously unknown to me.

My father and uncle were born in San Antonio, and it was there that the various grocery stores my grandfather had established from 1910 thru 1921, flourished and earned him a respectable living. In fact, a representative of a large grocery store approached my grandfather and proposed a partnership so that their company could expand to San Antonio. However, my grandfather turned down their offer, a decision he regretted to the day he died. By 1921, my grandfather was well established in Mexico pioneering the automobile and trucking industry in Mexico.

Once we were finished with the visiting of the relatives and the shopping, we hopped on a Texas regional airline that flew Convair aircraft and headed to Dallas Love Field to connect to another one bound for Little Rock. When we boarded our twin-prop plane, I was as excited as any kid would be, probably even more than on Christmas. I got to sit by the window, and my father was visibly very nervous about this trip. He appeared to be reasonably okay with the flight on the DC-6 from Mexico City, but this seemed very different flying with only two prop engines. I asked him what would happen if one of the prop engines gave out in the air. That was probably the wrong question to ask him at the wrong time and place to ask it! He was visibly perturbed by the question but answered immediately that the plane could fly on one engine until it landed safely. He seemed to have said that more for his own benefit than my own. That satisfied me and seemed to relax him more. He was particularly nervous upon take-off and landings, actually the most dangerous part of any flight on any aircraft. So, he wasn't too pleased when he found out in Love Field that our plane to Little Rock would be on a Convair 440 two-engine prop plane that would have two stops, one in Texarkana and the other in Hot Springs.

The flight attendant (stewardesses back then) had the most pronounced Texas twang I had ever heard. It was like she was singing Texas cowboy songs around the campfire. I could barely understand her. 'Would Y'all like a soda or somethin' chilled to drink?' Can you get any more exotic than that? And this was only Texas and Arkansas!

We arrived in Little Rock in the evening, as it practically took the whole day to travel from San Antonio, Texas to Little Rock, Arkansas through Dallas Love Field and towns in between. We went directly to a high-rise hotel in downtown Little Rock. It was air-conditioned, a luxury back then, and a prerequisite, as my father couldn't stand the heat. He blamed it on having spent years while stationed in Calcutta, India, during World War II, where the temperature was unbearable, and air-conditioning was an unknown. Thus, he luxuriated in the air-conditioned hotels in the States, even though they cost more than non-air-conditioned ones.

In Little Rock, we remembered I still had some clothing and other items that I needed which we had not had the opportunity to purchase in San Antonio. So, with directions from the hotel attendant, we hopped on a Little Rock transit bus that would take us to a nearby Sears. The coaches in Little Rock at that time weren't air-conditioned like the ones in San Antonio. My father was less than pleased. While on the bus, I witnessed something I had not ever seen before, not even in San Antonio.

On that slow, steamy bus there was an African-American woman sitting towards the front of the bus. A white man suddenly yelled at her to go to the back of the bus. She refused, and the driver threatened to stop the bus and throw the man off if he didn't stop harassing the woman. I whispered to my father, "why is that man so ugly to that woman." He whispered back, "I'll tell you later." He never did, and I never brought it up again. That was my first exposure to racism and discrimination. I never could understand it and still don't to this day.

The next day we traveled on a bus from Little Rock to the little town in northeast Arkansas. One of the brothers of St. Mathew School for Boys picked us up from the bus station and drove us to the school 9 miles west of town. It was in the middle of farmlands and wooded areas of dense tall old trees and brush. Brother Charles, the school's principal, and Superior led us on a brief but informative tour of the school. He asked some of the other students to take my suitcases to the main (and only) dormitory. It had about 80 beds in one large room. Meanwhile, Bro. Charles discussed money issues, tuition, permits, etc.

I stayed in the room with them part of the time to discuss my transition from a Spanish only educational system to an all English curriculum and to discuss the "rules" (my favorite subject). I was set back one year by Bro. Charles because they thought that the Mexican educational system was not up to U.S. standards. This actually proved to be the opposite. My education with the nuns at the orphanage and at the seminary was, by far, quite superior. But this simple decision by Bro. Charles, I was to learn later, would be the best decision he ever made. His decision set up a chain of events that would land me in the right class at High School. The best days of my life.

Bro. Charles's rules didn't seem too severe compared to what I was used to in the seminary. But I didn't like rules. Still, don't. But if anyone was going to abide by them, (for the most part), I was the one to reluctantly meet the requirements. One of the early learnings in my treasure chest of things to learn in this life was that most rules are made to be obeyed, and in the seminary, I was to follow them humbly without protest. Then there were the rules I loved to break and celebrate when I never got caught! I learned to yield instead of resisting. I found struggling against life's ordinances never worked. It's like trying to beat the river by swimming upstream. Why waste time and effort on something you're not going to win anyway? It reminds of the quote by Eckhart Tolle: "Whatever you fight, you strengthen, and what you resist, persists."

St. Mathew School took adjusting. I was shy and didn't make friends quickly, at least not right away. My first friends were the Spanish speakers of course. These were kids from Mexico, Central America and a few from Venezuela. In the early 1960's, Catholic Charities sent the school, at least a dozen freshly arrived Cuban refugees. They were mostly kids of wealthy Cuban parents who made the sacrifices to get their children out of Communist Cuba. We made quick friends, and they became my best friends. One of Bro. Charles's rules were *no Spanish*. But that was the one rule we loved to break. How can you tell me I can't speak my native tongue? However, the Anglo students were merciless when it came to the Spanish speakers. They called us *spics* and *wetbacks*, etc. Many of them sarcastically asked me "how come you're so white and you 'spic' like a Mexican?" It didn't take me long to learn to pronounce the English language correctly, but that didn't keep the bullying in abeyance.

My American school was the inauguration of a brand-new life for me! I loved spending my weekly allowance on Zeros, Buttermilks, M & M's, Milky Ways, etc. I learned all the new pop songs of the early 60's from the Little Rock AM radio station. My Cuban friends and I would sing them as if we were on stage in some fancy theatre with all of our fans yelling and screaming at us. We went on field trips and weekend movies to the Rialto Theatre, the only indoor movie theatre in the little Arkansas town. If we were lucky and our bonus money came in to buy clothes and other necessities, there was always the tiny J.C. Penney's and Sears.

My Cuban friends were extremely, clothing and accessories savvy and would not be undone by anyone else. Most of them were obsessed with their appearance. I wasn't too preoccupied with styles and clothing. But it seems like that's all they were concerned with. The school was also about watching American Television! I was introduced to The Ed Sullivan Show on Sunday Nights, Saturday or Sunday Night at the

Movies, Bonanza, American Bandstand on Saturday mornings. My new school introduced me to the cold frigid winters of the U.S. and the first snowfalls in my life.

It was there that I experienced the terrible events of November 22, 1963. Those are the dates in history when you remember where you were and what you were doing and the feelings that arose out of those horrid memories. I remember many of the parents of the Latin American kids canceled their child's tuition and had them sent home immediately. Puzzled by this strange occurrence, I asked Bro. Charles why my friends were leaving so suddenly. He explained that no amount of convincing by the Brothers that the U.S. was not going to have a revolution, prevented the parents of the kids from rescinding their marching orders. In Latin America, when a President was assassinated, that automatically meant that an uprising or revolution was forthcoming. I thought, how dumb is that! We never saw our friends again. That is the power of cultural paradigms.

St. Mathew School was a good anchor for me in the years of emotional anguish to come later in my life. But my next step in the long road of life and education in the U.S. was the real anchor that I cherish to this day. I attribute the experiences and happy memories the Catholic High School in Texas that I attended afterward, to literally saving my life. I refer back to it over and over again for the joy and the beautiful memories that it brought me. Those memories, like Mamanita and my stepmother Tere, were life vests thrown at me in the middle of an empty and tempestuous sea. My *Cosmic Team* saw to it that I had something to hang on to and that would keep me from floundering in the deep dark sea of desperation.

CHAPTER 15

MY PROUD AMERICAN HIGH SCHOOL

"Someday, after mastering the winds, the waves, the tides, and gravity, we shall harness for God the energies of love, and then, for a second time in the history of the world, man will have discovered fire."
~ Pierre Teilhard de Chardin

High School was the next step for me, St. Jerome High School in Texas. I arrived at SJHS cautiously optimistic, after all, now I was dealing with older kids and a different environment altogether than Jr. High School. I was fortunate to have a few friends from Mexico. I was housed with some of them in a large dormitory that was set up mainly for underclassmen. Brother Paul was our dorm Prefect. That was a year of stressful adjustment to a new and sometimes ominous environment for a teenager dealing with the challenges of puberty. I was clumsy in my relationships, especially with the upperclassmen, who tended to look down upon us younger students. But for the most part, I kept to myself and nurtured the friendships I could.

During my Sophomore year, I was bullied provoking severe anxiety and depression. It brought forth all the memories of the orphanage and curiously enough, the bullying came from a Mexican from Northern Mexico. He knew that I came from Mexico, and he taunted me every opportunity he had and almost always in front of his Mexican friends. I finally reached a point when I had to cry out for help. I went to Bro. Peter, our Principal, and I broke down in tears in his office. To this day, I can remember sitting in his office in front of his desk and unleashing my angst and anger. I couldn't stop the tears, the hurt, and the fear. He said to me: *"When they plunge the knife in they know how to twist it around don't they?"* Between sobs, I nodded in acknowledgment at my frustration at having to still deal with emotional and physical abuse.

Bro. Peter was one of the most understanding brothers that we had on our staff at SJHS, demonstrating genuine compassion and understanding. Bro. Peter shared stories from his youth about being bullied, and he appeared to understand my pain. He was not going to put up with it. From that day forward, the bullying stopped completely. I feared reprisals, but none happened.

For that same reason, I spent many a weekend going to San Antonio to stay at my great aunt's house. Aunt Alice enjoyed my visit, as did I. But she worried excessively. When I didn't come home early. Six pm was too late for her, especially when I went to the movies downtown and had to take the bus back to her house. So, that became a stressful situation in itself. In time, the trips to San Antonio became less frequent. They stopped the next year altogether as her health deteriorated. As time went on, the need to get away from campus became less urgent, especially after the bullying stopped.

My Junior and Senior years at SJHS were the highlights of my high school years. For the first time in my life, as a growing adolescent, I finally was accepted by my peers for who I was. My contributions to my school community were valued and respected. I joined clubs and organizations that I would have otherwise have stayed away from for fear of being rejected. I joined the school newspaper as a contributor. One could say that my writing career started then!

My Senior year was the culmination of excitement and accomplishment. I ran for a position on the Student Council and was elected vice-president, though I had longed for the president's job. However, I was satisfied. I could settle for that. I was proud of myself! I had been accepted by my peers! They wanted me to represent them.

I loved going to our football games, and Homecoming night was an exceptional night. All the classes built a float, and the school obtained a city permit to parade our floats in the city streets. Wow! It didn't get any better than that! I was chosen to escort our homecoming queen. Our picture was splashed on the front cover of The Sentinel, our school newspaper. Sometimes, I just didn't quite know how to handle myself. I was filled with a sense of accomplishment, in this case, social achievement, a significant life event for me.

My Junior and Senior years of high school taught me that I could lead when empowered to do so. I learned that I was acceptable as well as accepted. I know that sounds strange, but understanding where I had come from, it was like reaching the peak of Mr. Everest.

I so enjoyed the music from the 1960's. I enjoyed the sock hops and the proms. I enjoyed being part of the mainstream movers and shakers. But I don't remember myself being stuck up or distant from my peers, on the contrary, I always intended to be of service. Not surprising since one of my best friends, Mark and I, were awarded a Special Service Award at our graduation. I made the National Honor Society and was given other awards as well. The years at SJHS were the days of my recovery from rejection and abject abandonment. I had found my family! Graduation day was a day of incredible celebration and happiness and at the same time a terrible day. It was sad because it meant I had to leave my friends and my school community. We were the last graduating class of SJHS. We were the class that closed the doors on a long tradition.

It wasn't until many years later, 40 years at least, that I would learn why the years at St. Jerome's High School were given to me as an individual gift from Spirit. It's hard to explain, but when depression tackles one's ability to keep afloat, it takes a special lifesaver to be thrown at you to be able to survive the tempestuous seas. In one of those phases of intense fear and anxiety due to the effects of PTSD, it happened that the stress was so extreme and stressful that I entered in what is called a dissociative state. Familiar environments and people were no longer familiar. It gave me a sense of being lost and without an identity to cling to. I felt stripped of the beingness that was so familiar to me. It felt like I was outside of my body looking at a psychedelic movie of myself in an unfamiliar environment. This first event happened in the midst of my total immersion in the cult, and it was utterly surreal and caused me deep anxiety. It was like I was on a continuous LSD intravenous drip, a dangerous trip indeed.

This repeated itself many years after the cult. However, the frequency of events decreased as years went on. On some of these occasions, it got so intense that I had to have something with which to reclaim my sense of identity and familiarity. So, I made copies of pictures from my High School yearbooks, and I posted these all over my living space: on the refrigerator, on the walls of my bedroom, on my bathroom mirror. I remember closing my eyes, and while I listened to my favorite music from the sixties, I visualized myself back in those days, the conversations, the dances and sock hops, the school events, etc. It was only when I was able to barely grasp hold of a sliver of reality that eventually it became stronger and stronger. This allowed me to merge back to normalcy which decreased the anxiety and discomfort.

When Spirit sends us a life vest or a survival instrument, it is meant to give us support in time of turbulence. These memories are the lifeboats that we climb into, soaked to the bones, trembling with hypothermic fear to rescue us from certain calamity. These survival markers are not just memories, they can present themselves as people, books, inspiring moments of awakened wisdom, or any form of the liberation from life's tempests. But we have to learn to recognize them and take advantage of them.

PART II

THE LONG ROAD TO RECOVERY

CHAPTER 16

THE COMING IN AND THE GOING OUT

"A problem well-stated is half-solved."
~ Charles Kettering

When I finally made it home to my sister and brother-in-law's house, they were delighted to see me and celebrated my return. I was glad to be home and safe. But in the back of my mind, I had the memory of that horrible nightmare. I wondered whether it really happened. Could it be true? Everything was normal at home with my relatives. I savored my new-found safety. I was like a battered ship in a storm-tossed sea that had found refuge. I was in port, and it was safe. I adapted as best I could, and I thanked my sister and brother-in-law profusely for permitting me to stay with them. I found it difficult to direct their questions away from a compelling need to spill my guts and tell them the horrors I had experienced. I knew that if I talked about it, I would run the risk of awakening the iguana that laid in wait.

Now when I speak of the iguana, I want to be sure that we are aware of what that symbolizes. As mentioned before, the iguana is nothing more than a figurative representation of the Limbic System of the brain that houses the Fight/Flight/Freeze Response (FFFR) that was referred to earlier. It is often referred to as the reptilian or primitive brain. The organ responsible for sounding the bells and whistles of danger is called the amygdala. The amygdala is an almond-shaped organ, one in each hemisphere of the brain. Amygdala means almond in Greek. The amygdalae are also processors of memory and more specifically of emotional memories. They alert us to danger, whether real or imagined.

When danger is detected the adrenal glands secrete the primary stress hormones namely: adrenaline, norepinephrine, and cortisol. All three are responsible for various activities that help the system survive. These include: shunting blood to the center part of the body to protect the critical organs. This action also enables tissue repair should that become necessary. Stress hormones increase our blood pressure and heart rate to be able to fight or flee, an increase blood supply to muscles such as the leg and arm muscles facilitates the fight or flight process. It suspends critical functions such as reproduction (sperm production or ovulation), tissue repair, and digestion. Why digest lunch if you might become lunch!

Animals produce the same stress hormones when they are threatened or under attack. The good thing about the FFFR in animals is that once the danger passes they resume doing what they were doing. Animals don't ruminate about what might have happened to them, like: "Oh, that stupid idiotic lion! How dare him to come after me! Doesn't he know how important I am", and on and on. Animals don't engage in that sort of dialogue. But for us humans it's different. We can't seem to turn off the FFFR, and we ruminate and re-experience the trauma over and over again, sometimes for life.

The Limbic system is not responsible for critical thinking skills, such as analysis or contemplation, that task belongs to the prefrontal cortex. So, when we think of a past stressful event, the limbic system interprets that event as happening in the present moment, and the FFFR is launched. That event releases the stress hormones referred to earlier which creates a reinforcing effect and that in turn makes the incident fresher and eventually more alarming. Through repeated action, the disturbing episode that happened long ago is reinforced, and the reminiscence of it is recorded in our memory banks which in turn is intricately tied in with the Amygdala. This unfortunate condition in most cases turns into Post-Traumatic Stress Disorder (PTSD), and or other anxiety disorders. Although that's how the stress mechanism works, that doesn't necessarily mean that it can't be reversed or disarmed. We will talk about ways to do that later.

One of the first things that I did was to make a conscious intention to make a new life out my current existence. That meant only one thing: start over again! I reflected on what my mission might possibly be on this earth. What was I to do with myself? How was I going to be of service to others? How could I be of assistance to others when I was lugging around all the lies and deceptions from the TG's sick and deranged mind? I couldn't. So, there was only one thing to do, and that was to get rid of it as best I knew how. Burn all the materials, the books, and publications that I had brought with me. I couldn't just dump everything when I left the Pacific Northwest; I still had to hang on to my programming. I suppose, in retrospect, that was a healthy thing to do. But, I resolved to be done with it all. So, I took all the books and papers from the cult and went to the backyard and opened the B-B-Q pit and I burned everything! That was the first significant step I took. The next step was to avoid feeding the iguana with the thoughts that triggered the anxiety, in other words, avoid telling more stories.

I had to develop a system to dismantle the ugly belief system that I had acquired. When I left the cult, I went with bundles of fear and anxiety. I anxiously ruminated about the fear-based concepts I internalized. I could hear the leaders of the sect say horrible evil things that would happen to us if we disobeyed and abandoned the cause. My whole life was completely turned upside down. I didn't know what to do other than try to lead as healthy a life as possible. The fear and anxiety took their toll on my mental and emotional health. It was at this time that I determined that my experiences with that religion were not going to ruin my life anymore. I vowed I would not let it destroy me.

I swore that the mentally ill cult leader would no longer contaminate my mind with vile poison. Once I made up my mind, I initiated an arduous path of normalization, of deprogramming, of confronting the beliefs and ideas that consumed me. I revisited the books from the organization that existed decades before and which I mentioned in the chapter on my exit from the sect. I used that information to deprogram the schizophrenic lies of the cult leaders I had left behind. Positive thinking, as opposed to negative thinking, was emphasized. So, that began the whole process of restricting my awareness and developing a very mindful, almost fatiguing, alertness to how I directed the energies of my attention.

As I was going through my self-deprogramming process, I became more and more aware of my thought processes and how they related to my feelings. As I look back, it wasn't an easy lesson, but it was invaluable. I became so acutely aware of the power of my thoughts. I was profoundly conscious of the subversive hypnotic tactics and suggestions that literally wrapped their tentacles around our brains, our minds, and our whole psyche. I reflected once again, how my cult-mates had become zombies walking around in a daze enveloped in mantles of fear and anxiety. These individuals were so consumed by depression and dissociative states that they walked around like robots at the beck and call of the vicious and despotic cult lieutenants. We led joyless lives. I was completely zapped of energy and seemingly devoid of resources.

I thought to myself: "How could I have possibly fallen for this!" "What got into me?" As I reflect back, I know that I had an excellent lesson to learn. I had to go through a truly extraordinary experience to enable me to grow and learn. I had to learn the power of thought. I had to learn how thinking can become a terrifying weapon that can destroy lives and rob people of their life, their joy, and, in some cases, their very existence. But I also learned that the power of thought goes beyond creating chaos and was, in fact, the liberating force that finally set me free. I also learned the damage that fear-based beliefs unleash in the psyches of human beings. I learned that I should never instill fear in any human being, no matter how trivial the fear may appear to be.

I realized that I felt terrible when I entertained a specific idea or group of thoughts. These ideas provoked anxious feelings, and when I didn't feed them with my attention, the anxiety dissipated. It was then that I realized that our minds lie to us more often than not. They create stories upon stories that, when all is said and done, and when the flow of the nasty deluge of delusions stops, we become peaceful.

One of my spiritual counselors a few years ago once told me that when we hear fear-based stories or other fear-based thoughts, we set them aside and observe them from a distance. We soon see them for what they are: just stories. People love to tell stories. They learn stories from other people and those other people heard those stories from still others, and so on. All in vain do the stories reflect the truth. Stories are propagated by other storytellers. And the stories they tell change with each story-teller. Not a foolproof way to replicate a story and keep to its original version, is it?

Just because the millions of people in pre-1492 Europe believed that the Earth was flat, people would die for that truth. Sailors refused to sail beyond the sight of the land for fear of being eaten by the dragons of the sea or fall off the edge of the earth. Those dragons were real within the confines of their brains. But as we gaze at our magnificent and endangered planet from outer space, we realize that truth always prevails in spite of the story-tellers and their untrue stories, in spite of the liars and their lies.

To quote B. Katie: "Who would you be without your story? You never know until you inquire. There is no story that is you or that leads to you. Every story leads away from you. Turn it around; undo it. You are what exists before all stories."

As I look back at those deranged storytellers that turned my life temporarily upside down, I do everything in my power to have compassion for them knowing that they were the believers of falsehoods told by other storytellers.

CHAPTER 17

THE POWER OF OPPOSITES: MY FIRST BREAKTHROUGH

"Light is meaningful only in relation to darkness, and truth presupposes error. It is these mingled opposites which people our life, which make it pungent, intoxicating. We only exist regarding this conflict, in the zone where black and white clash."
~Louis Aragon

"Contraria Sunt Complementa." — *"Opposites are Complementary."*
~Niels Bohr, Danish Physicist

I was working as a lead trainer for one of the U.S Department of Education's Training Center that worked with schools and communities in the prevention of alcohol and drug abuse. Our continuing education curriculum was rich with new and fresh information, not just on substance abuse prevention, but on essential human skill development, from conflict resolution to useful communication skills. We traveled throughout our territory and trained teachers to become trainers in their own right. The trainees then trained other teachers, who in turn, would help kids develop refusal skills in dealing with drugs and alcohol. It was a vital prevention program, with state-of-the-art information and practices. At that time in my life, I was living a barren life without any spiritual routines to speak of, except Meditation, which I am so grateful I never abandoned. Religion had become a poison for me, especially new age teachings. When one wanders through a spiritual desert, seemingly alone, one still gets thirsty for the sustenance that Spirit brings to our souls.

One of our trainers and best friend Beverly introduced me to an excellent program to help me understand myself better, to understand others better and to strengthen my relationships. This was the first program or body of information that helped me to truly understand what happened to me and why I ventured far off the path. The Opposite Strengths program enabled me to understand why humans do bad things to themselves and to others. It opened my eyes to some of the reasons why I may have accepted the cult that sent me into depression and despair. As a matter of fact, it explicitly laid out the patterns that I most would respond to and which would put me in harm's way.

It helped me to understand that I had strengths, and if I overused those strengths, I would experience problems in my life. The 2-day program was created by Dr. Jay Thomas and carried on by his son Dr. Tommy Thomas. This program was a Godsend for me. I would consider it another life-raft placed at my disposal by Spirit to rescue me from drowning in an unforgiving sea of fear and trepidation.

To quote Dr. Tommy Thomas: "The Opposite Strengths program flows from one simple, central idea: Personal growth, creativity, productivity, and effectiveness result from the blending, or interaction, of two opposite strengths." The two strengths have equal values and are in perfect opposition to one another – much like the Yin is to the Yang. As a matter of fact, the Chinese adhered to the principles of the Tai Chi (symbol of yin and yang) centuries before these concepts were even contemplated by Western thinkers and philosophers.

The core of our personality is made of the following strengths:

- The basic pair   – **Thinking** and **Risking**
- The thinking pair – **Practical Thinking** and **Theoretical Thinking**
- The risking pair   – **Dependent Risking** and **Independent Risking**

Dr. Thomas says that although each strength has equal value, they are opposite and different. Each strength interacts with each other in a creative dance of feeding off of the other. Thinking leads to Risking and Risking leads back to reflect on Thinking. The same applies to the other pairs, both the risking pair and the thinking pair. Each one of the strengths feeds the other, and it causes a chain reaction of creativity and productivity.

Each of us has all of the strengths; we use each strength on a daily basis. But like being left handed or right handed, we tend to use one strength more than the other. Thus, from the combination of all the strengths emerge 8 patterns of core strengths. Patterns 1 thru 4 lead from Thinking and patterns 5 thru 8 lead from Risking. In this first 2-day workshop my eyes were opened to a brand-new understanding of what my strengths were and how the overuse of these strengths led me to the labyrinth of toxic belief systems.

To find out what my core strengths were, I filled out a detailed questionnaire on myself and five other people who knew me very well also filled out the same questionnaire. The scores of the self-questionnaire were averaged with the five-person questionnaire. Each represents fifty percent of one's total score. From the averages emerge one's primary core pattern and a supporting flex pattern or secondary pattern. When I was given my rating, I nearly fell out of my chair. I came out as a Pattern 6 with a Pattern 5 as a secondary. That means that I lead from Risking, I am a Theoretical Thinker and a Dependent Risker.

That was the perfect combination to make me ripe to be sucked into a non-evidenced based belief system such as the vile cult that would haunt my life for many years to follow. Although Dr. Thomas does not assign any other qualities or dimensions to Theoretical Thinking, for me and my experiences with the cult, I discovered that the Theoretical Thinking strength branched out into two broad camps: Evidenced-based Theoretical Thinking and Non-Evidenced based Theoretical Thinking. Evidence-based Theoretical Thinking is demonstrated by scientists, physicists, or any individual who relies primarily on the scientific methods of observation and measurement to arrive at a theory. In simple terms: it's research-based. This would be similar to the theory of relativity, the theory of evolution, and the theories of quantum physics. Here is a quote from HowStuffWorks that illustrates this quite clearly:

"A scientific theory often seeks to synthesize a body of evidence or observations of particular phenomena. It's generally — though by no means always — a grander, testable statement about how nature operates. You can't necessarily reduce a scientific theory to a pithy statement or equation, but it does represent something fundamental about how nature works."

Non-Evidence based theoretical thinking is any belief system that is not based on evidence but just forms part of the person's free will to believe in something even though there is no evidence to support its validity.

Furthermore, in the program, I learned that when we overuse our strengths, we create a condition known as Polarization. It occurs when we misuse our core strengths or overemphasize them to the point where we get stuck in that strength. Polarization sets up a blockage of the benefits that originate from the opposite supporting strength. For example, thinking led to risking and vice versa risking leads back to thinking. This pair is linked by a horizontal figure 8 that ties both opposites together. However, in polarization, a block is set up between the pairs at the nexus of the figure eight, and the opposite supporting strengths expressions is effectively blocked. This creates a severe imbalance. Human creativity and productivity come from the blend and interaction of both opposite strengths. When there is a block, creativity is cut off, and we become stale and stagnated. For example, the symptoms of polarization in theoretical thinking are the following in a person:

+ "Continue to imagine possibilities when it's time to <u>look at the facts</u>;
+ The build-up of ideas and possibilities;
+ Possibilities become increasingly important;
+ Sees the pot of gold at the end of the rainbow;
+ Eager to try something new;
+ Facts are a threat;
+ Sees all the reasons why an idea will work;
+ Disregard facts;
+ Unbridled optimism;
+ Imagination runs wild;
+ Flights of fantasy;
+ Loses contact with reality;
+ Lives in a dream world."

(Thomas, J.W. EdD; Thomas, Tommy, Ph.D., <u>The Power of Opposite Strengths</u>, Page 143, Figure 9).

Since I led from my Risking strength the signs of becoming polarized on Risking are:

+ "Continues to engage in action when it's time to <u>stop and think</u>;
+ The build-up of activity and movement;
+ Action becomes increasingly important;
+ Thinks less and less;
+ Expresses feelings aggressively;
+ Resists thoughtful analysis;
+ Quick to change things;
+ Makes quick decisions;
+ Feels increasingly exposed and agitated;
+ Becomes more and more emotional;
+ Out of control."

(Thomas, J.W. EdD; Thomas, Tommy, Ph.D., <u>The Power of Opposite Strengths</u>, Page 140, Figure 8).

Furthermore, since I also led from Dependent Risking these were the signs I was polarized on this strength:

- "Continues to depend on others when it is time to depend on self;
- The build-up of support and approval of others;
- Support and approval of others become increasingly important;
- Fewer and fewer expressions of independence;
- Says *yes* when should say *no*;
- Becomes less and less responsible;
- Loses self-confidence;
- Loses awareness of self;
- Loses the respect of others;
- Finally, loses the support and approval of others the very thing that is most dear."

(Thomas, J.W. EdD; Thomas, Tommy, Ph.D., <u>The Power of Opposite Strengths</u>, Page 147, Figure 10).

So, the above painted my rather grim predisposition to fall for a belief system without questioning its validity, the integrity of the leaders, or the ultimate reality of the results that that belief system might produce. I was polarized on Risking – I jumped in without questioning who, what, when, where, how come, as evidenced by not taking my time to carefully analyze the principles of the cult or how it was affecting people already in it. More importantly, I was not paying attention to how the dogmas being panhandled by the cultists made me feel, which, eventually, were feelings of fear and desperation.

I was polarized on Dependent risking – I wanted to feel accepted and people pleasing was very easy for me. I became overconfident about other's opinions and their absolute belief that the cult was the cradle of truth. I went along with the crowd without asking where we are going, what we are going to do when we get there, and how I would feel once we arrived.

The Polarization of non-Theoretical thinking (especially non-evidenced based) led me to accept just about anything that anyone said to me as the absolute truth without verifying any form of evidence or research. Then, I wondered why I got myself into such a mess!

The Opposite Strengths program opened my eyes. It showed me how quickly an imbalance in the expression of my strengths, which are intrinsically positive, can lead to such disarray in my life. I knew from the program that to prevent further polarization I had to emphasize my opposite polar supporting strengths. So, for risking, it was critical for me to stress my thinking strength. In other words, it was vital for me to think before risking - think things through and hold back on taking any action until it was entirely safe to do so. It would've been beneficial for me to question proposals or thoughts from others and refrain from making decisions without thoroughly analyzing the issue(s). Another disadvantage in those days was the lack of the internet to go online and conduct research of the organization and any legal actions taken against it, or just be able to look up participant reviews in general. All of that would've been an immense help.

For Theoretical Thinking, it is essential to distinguish between evidence-based and non-evidence based Thinking. Evidence-based Theoretical Thinking relies on the scientific method of observations and measurements to arrive at theories of probabilities. For example, quantum theory, or the theory of relativity are based upon scientific inquiry. Non-evidenced based theoretical thinking, on the other hand, is not based upon evidence (although there may be some circumstantial facts presented,) but instead on belief and supposition. For example, the non-evidence theoretical thinkers are people who invent concepts and ideas without any substantiation of these constructs. They subscribe to ideas and beliefs that are passed down as tradition, legends or folklore, or just pure faith.

If that thought were to be subjected to the scientific method, then the following questions would have to be answered: Have these phenomena been observed and measured? How were these phenomena observed? What instruments were used? What was the detected energy pattern of these phenomena? What were the effects of these energy patterns? How did these energy patterns interact in the immediate or distant environments? Have the singularities been duplicated in a laboratory setting with the same results? Have these studies been subjected to peer reviews? Etc. One can imagine the fumbling and mumbling of these individuals when asked these questions.

They would be unable to answer them. The reason is the phenomena in question have never been observed or measured. <u>In essence, the ideas exist only within the cranial boundaries of the believers of those thoughts, and not outside of those boundaries</u>. Polarization on Theoretical Thinking leads to some very unpleasant human scenarios. As a matter of fact, Dr. Thomas says that extreme forms of polarization can, and do, on many occasions, lead to physical death. I evidently succumbed to non-evidenced based Theoretical Thinking. This caused me much suffering and pain. Thankfully, I didn't lose my life.

The antithesis or the opposite expression of Theoretical Thinking is Practical Thinking. Practical Thinking helps us to get grounded and pushes us to look at the facts and the evidence that supports *what is* as opposed to *what could be*. Practical Thinking demands proof and evidence through observation or measurement. Practical Thinking and Theoretical Thinking feed each other, especially when it comes to the formulation of scientific theorems.

One of my strategies to overcome my overdose of non-evidence based theoretical thinking was to delve into science and nature. I read all the physics books for laymen that I could get my hands on and that helped to get anchored in the here and now. My head was firmly planted on this earth and not swimming in some otherworldly broth of idiotic ideas. One of those first books I read was the Tao of Physics by Fritjof Capra. What an excellent synthesis of science and spirituality! It taught me that science and spirituality are not only compatible but one and the same.

I reverted (flexed) to my Independent Risking strength and refused to permit anyone to do my thinking for me. I refused to "go along" and vehemently protested stupid and unsubstantiated ideas. I questioned religion and religious beliefs but did so without abandoning my essential spirituality, my faith in an Infinite, Indescribable Higher Wisdom and Power. I consider religion one thing and spirituality quite another. Religion to me is the practice of adhering to a set of ritualistic paradigms (that are mostly represented by non-evidence based Theoretical Thinking) and most of the time require strict adherence by their membership. Religion is binding, and in many cases, rigid and inflexible.

The definition of religion by Merriam-Webster is: "The service and worship of God or the supernatural (2): commitment or devotion to religious faith or observance; (3): a personal set or institutionalized system of religious attitudes, beliefs, and practices."

The more polarized religions are, the more exclusive they tend to become. You are discriminated against and hated for who you are. The apologists go around preaching to the world: "*Oh we love the sinner but hate the 'sin.'*" First of all, WHO gave you the right to hate anybody or anything? Certainly, not the person you follow, whether that be Jesus, or Buddha, or the Tao, etc. From what we know of the person known as Jesus, he hated no one, but loved everyone <u>unconditionally</u> and accepted everyone <u>unconditionally</u>. The dictionary definition of unconditional is: "not limited by conditions." He was (and is) the ensoulment of absolute unconditional love, peace, and compassion.

To me, there is only one religion. That religion is pure Divine Unconditional Love. We are genuine love and are capable of showing it or demonstrating it every day of our lives with everybody that we come in contact with. Yes, that includes the person who cut you off or tailgated you all the way home. Spirituality, for me, is to practice silence and stillness in the sentience of an infinite sea of oneness and unity. It is my relationship with nature and that which IS. Spirituality to me is Meditation and awareness of consciousness and being consciously aware. Spirituality to me also means practicing present moment awareness or, commonly known as, mindfulness. Spirituality is being aware of my relationships and how to improve upon them.

A critical aspect of the polarization that affected my life, and perhaps this may be true for Polarization in general, was that it reached such a point of massive build-up that it reverted back to its opposing expression.

Let me give you an example of this from my own experience. (1). I became polarized on Risking (impulsively subscribing to a belief system without questioning its validity); (2). I was polarized on Dependent Risking (not daring to interrogate authority for fear of not being accepted by them and refusing to go against the crowd); and most importantly, (3).

I became polarized on Theoretical Thinking (principally, non-evidence based Theoretical Thinking by believing absurd, unproven theories). Once I reached critical mass, my whole worldview shifted 360 degrees.

I flexed to my Thinking Strength and made a point to think things through thoroughly before taking action. I flexed to my Practical Thinking Strength by being more aware of _what is_ as opposed to _what could be_. I did this by studying every layman's book on physics and science. I reviewed the antithesis of religious belief systems and brought down the hollow idols of gurus and teachers. I emphasized more, my Independent, Risking Strength by not going along with the crowd and saying no when it was necessary to do so.

More importantly, I made a firm stand that I would not permit other people to do my thinking for me. And finally, I learned to flex to my opposite supporting strength of Independent Risking by refusing to accept point blank what others said and firmly held my ground in refusing to go along just because it was so vital for me to be recognized and not be turned away.

The Opposite Strengths program was the beginning of my complete unlearning process. I had to learn to unlearn the toxic beliefs that poisoned my life. I had a rational explanation why people do ugly things to other people or why they kill people in mass killings. I had a backup belief system supported by evidence and systematic academic studies. That was firm ground for me. I had a logical explanation of the whys and wherefores of human injustices and cruel acts from a behavioral standpoint as opposed to a superstitious and fearful one, such as the ludicrous explanation that evil spirits were to blame. It felt so good!

I highly recommend that you purchase a copy of the Power of Opposite Strengths. Attending an Opposite Strengths Seminar or Opposite Strengths Executive Coaching experience would significantly enhance your internalization of the information to change your life for the better.

For more information visit: www.oppositestrengths.com

CHAPTER 18

WHAT ARE PARADIGMS?

"There is nothing either good or bad
but thinking makes it so."
~ William Shakespeare

"The world is nothing but my perception of it. I see only
through myself. I hear only through the filter of my story."
~ B. Katie

I still ask myself today why my Seminary superiors could not see the incident with the poor woman and her baby from a different viewpoint. Why couldn't they have stopped and thought out a more reasonable response to a 13-year-old still in the early stages of physical and intellectual development? Why the *stuckness*? Why the inflexibility? I think it all had to do with their paradigms or mental models. Did it have anything to do with perhaps the same obstinacy and stubbornness of the Church of Galileo that condemned him for his scientific observations of Heliocentrism, that the earth revolves around the sun and not the other way around? Galileo was declared a heretic by the Inquisition and was forced to recant his *heresy* and was imprisoned for the rest of his life. That is the power of paradigms and more specifically of paradigm paralysis.

I was conducting training in the 80's and 90's for the U.S. Department of Education's Regional Training Center, and I saw a video by Joel Barker called the Business of Paradigms. Although the video was created more for the business community, it had a profound influence on me to help me understand this whole business of cults, cultism and toxic beliefs systems, in general.

According to Willis Harmon, in <u>An Incomplete Guide to the Future,</u> "A paradigm is the basic way of perceiving, thinking, valuing, and doing. Thus: a paradigm is a set of rules and regulations that does two things: (1) it establishes and defines boundaries; and (2) it tells you how to behave inside those boundaries to be successful. Words that represent subsets of the paradigm concept: theory, model, methodology, principles, standards, protocol, routines, assumptions, conventions, patterns, habits, common sense, conventional wisdom, mindset, values, frames of reference, traditions, customs, prejudices, ideology, inhibitions, superstitions, rituals, compulsions, addictions, doctrine, dogma, cults, cultism."

In late 1992, I was working as a trainer/consultant for the U.S. Embassy in El Salvador. All U.S. consultants and Embassy personnel were under strict security protection as the war still waged on. At the time, rumors of a peace accord were circulating among the populace, so the fighting between the government and the rebels was theoretically winding down, even though we could still hear bombs explode in the nearby mountains surrounding the Capital.

The day before, I met with a war-weary group of officials from the Ministry of Education at a favorite restaurant in downtown San Salvador. We were planning the 5-day training event. I was charged with training a group of Salvadoran teachers in school leadership and substance abuse prevention. Suddenly and without warning, a loud bang could be heard on the street in front of the restaurant. Apparently, an old car backfired with a sizeable ball of smoke. Instinctively, and with surprising immediacy, everyone in the restaurant, except me, dove to the floor in a panic and scurried under the tables.

I looked around perplexed by this strange behavior. However, the people were responding to the amygdalae, which sounded the alarms that a bomb had gone off, one of many missiles that preceded this innocent bang. It demonstrated to me the profound effect war can have on an otherwise peaceful people. It was at that point that I realized this training took on a whole different meaning. I would have to deal with the trauma of war and its terrible effect on the citizens of El Salvador. I knew instinctively that they were in search of answers. Why did this war start? Why did we have the polarization that occurred? What was at the base of it? One of the topics was about paradigms, how they are formed, the role they played and how it influences human behavior. I played a video on Paradigms which explained how humans develop these mental models in their minds that, perhaps devoid of fact or reality, become the "truth" for those entertaining those paradigms.

When the video was over, I could see many of the participants smiling, with some writing furiously in their notebooks. Puzzled by their reactions, I asked for feedback about the video. The majority of them expressed elatedly that they could now put a face on the ugly monster that had terrified them. They understood that paradigms are mental models that directly influence human behavior, and some in a very profound way.

A few comments that I overheard at the break was: "Oh now I understand, the devil had nothing to do with this, and it's all a matter of ideas gone wrong." "Oh, God wasn't really punishing us, it had to do with paradigms." It was my impression at the time that the Salvadorian people were very religious.

The whole concept of paradigms explains how humans create a view of reality based on their mental constructs or models. These, most likely have been formulated from belief systems, from theoretical (evidenced based and non-evidenced based) constructs, imposed by parents, wives, husbands, priests, pastors, societal belief systems, superstitions, etc. In turn, these are mental models that become very real to the mind's inner eye.

So, once the paradigm is established, it creates boundaries. Within those boundaries are a set of rules and regulations that dictate a pattern upon which to act. It then creates a filtered view of the world colored by that paradigm. This is what I call the paradigm filtering system. William Glasser explained it as filters that are set up to produce an interpretation of observation (whether internally in mind or externally through the senses). These filters are the knowledge filter (what we know or what we have been taught), the sensory filter (sight, smell, hearing, touch, or taste) and the value filter or the meaning that we assign the information. This could be positive, negative or neutral, all based on the photo album of what we want to create. It also refers to what we value and what we do not want to give up or negotiate away.

In my experience within the cult, when the dust settled and I realized that I was deceived, manipulated, lied to, and robbed; I had to unlearn what I had learned and released the tremendous storehouse of emotional and mental energy which I had invested in those belief systems. One of the most challenging entanglements was the paradigm filtering effect. In polarized or radicalized thinking systems, the main strength which is overused is the Thinking Strength, and more specifically, and in this case, the non-evidence based Theoretical Thinking Strength.

When I was working in the criminal justice system, I conducted an informal study of 289 high-risk offenders who went through the Opposite Strengths Program. What would you guess was the principal Strength that the majority of those offenders overemphasized and eventually got polarized on? One would imagine Risking, but actually, the majority led from Thinking! This confirmed that their behaviors were the result of their criminal thinking which preceded their unlawful practices. However, in spite of their criminal pre-disposition, I found, surprisingly, that the younger high-risk offenders were more flexible in their cultural paradigms than, the older ones. An excellent example of this was when the issue of sexual orientation came up in group discussions. Most male younger offenders did not discriminate (at least openly in the group) against LGBTQ offenders, although male offenders tended to be less open about their sexuality than the female offenders. LGBTQ males have learned that society is not very forgiving of their sexuality. Females, on the other hand, were observed to be more open, tolerant and accepting of their gay companions or acquaintances.

On one occasion, a male participant in my Cognitive program voiced disparaging remarks about gays and lesbians. His operating paradigm was that sexuality was a choice. Therefore gays and lesbians should be responsible for their decision to be, in his words, *deviant*. I immediately challenged that paradigm by asking the whole group if they remembered where they were and what they were doing on 9/11 when the U.S. was attacked by Muslim radicals. The majority of the group raised their hand affirming positively that they knew exactly where they were and what they were doing. I emphasized that they probably knew all that information because that day was a very impressionably tragic one in our nation's history. So, I followed up that statement with the following: "So, you must also remember when you were younger and coming into your own sexual awareness, and you were perhaps sitting in your living room or at your kitchen table, and you had to make a critical decision in your life." I paused to let the sentence sink in, giving them a chance to ponder my statement.

The group steadily peered at me with a questioning, quizzical look on their faces. I then followed it up with a statement: "Then you must remember the day when you had to make the decision about whether you were going to be straight, gay, bisexual, or transgender." There was complete silence. One of the participants yelled out, "I didn't make a choice, I just knew that I was straight." I slowly glanced around the room in silence, and then I said very slowly: "I rest my case" ……. again, the group fell into complete silence. Everyone, without exception, just stared at me. Some shook their heads in agreement with an *I-see-your-point* look. No further questioning ever came out about that topic again. I repeated the same scenario with every Cognitive-Behavioral group I had if the issue ever came up. Most always, I saw the same outcome. As can be expected, there were a few group members wholly entrenched in Paradigm Paralysis. But, hopefully, the majority made an essential paradigm shift.

Less than two weeks after Hurricane Katrina, Pat Robertson implied on the September 12th broadcast of the 700 Club that the hurricane was God's punishment in response to America's abortion policy. He suggested that 9/11 and the disaster in New Orleans "could... be connected in some way". Of course, he wasn't the only one to chime in. Other radicals explained in their profound "I-know-what-I'm-talking-about" mode that Katrina hit New Orleans because of its ambiance of debauchery and lasciviousness.

Other polarized individuals, not just the Christians, threw their 2 cents in as well. Ovadia Yosef, a prominent ultra-Orthodox Israeli rabbi, declared that Hurricane Katrina to be "God's punishment for President Bush's support of the August 2005 withdrawal of Jewish settlers from the Gaza strip". He added that black people died because they did not study the Torah! Trump would blame it on President Barrack Obama or Hillary Clinton. The ridiculous list goes on. The problem is that these individuals not just propagated those beliefs, but they actually believed them! These are all examples of the *Paradigm Filtering Effect*. Beliefs are washed and colored by the observers' current ideas about the world, even though that observation is tainted with errors.

Cults and other toxic belief systems feed on lies and misrepresentation of the facts. One of the aspects of faulty thinking, as taught in Cognitive Behavioral therapy, is the phenomena of thinking errors. The above arguments are cluttered with thinking errors, and the most frequent thinking errors are jumping to conclusions or illogical thinking, making false statements and swearing allegiance to a truth that does not exist, like *fake news*.

One of the most helpful quotes that I read as I was going through my recovery/deprogramming process was a quote from Chapter 23 of the Tao Te Ching (translation by Mitchell):

"Be like the forces of nature:

When it blows, there is ONLY wind.

When it rains, there is ONLY rain.

When the clouds pass, the sun shines through."

To me, that meant that when things happen there is <u>NO</u> interpretation of those events and is just what it is. What is, is, and that's all there is. Or as Gary Zugav wrote in <u>The Dancing Wu Li Masters</u>: "God's in His heaven, and all's well with the world, except that according to the enlightened view, the world couldn't be any other way. It is neither well nor not well. It simply is what it is. What it is, is perfectly what it is. It couldn't be anything else. It is perfect. I am exactly and perfectly who I am. You are perfect. You are exactly and perfectly who you are. If you are a happy person, then that is what you perfectly are – a happy person. If you are an unhappy person, then that is what you perfectly are – an unhappy person. If you are a person who is changing, then that is what you perfectly are – a person who is changing. That which is - is that which is. That which is not is that which is. There is nothing which is not that which is. There is nothing other than that which is. Everything is that, which is. We are a part of that which is. In fact, we are that which is." (<u>Dancing Wu Li Masters</u>, Page 297-298).

That is why evidential (or research-based) thinking is such a threat to these belief systems and to their propaganda machines. The absurdity of their claims is automatically obliterated by facts. Facts or Practical Thinking is the first and foremost enemy of non-evidenced based Theoretical Thinking. Apologists are terrified of evidential facts and many will act-out angrily when confronted with the evidence. Some resort to violence because their whole world view is being threatened. In that case, the entire construct of their reality threatens to tumble down like a house of cards.

The whole argument of Intelligent Design is a perfect example of this non-evidenced based theoretical thinking model. "Intelligent Design (ID) is the pseudoscientific view that "certain features of the universe and of living things are best explained by an intelligent cause, not an undirected process such as natural selection. Educators, philosophers, and the scientific community have demonstrated that ID is a religious argument, a form or creationism which lacks empirical support and offers no testable or tenable hypothesis." (Wikipedia).

When a paradigm does not conform to the ID view of reality or any set of beliefs, apologists will then do everything they can to modify or adapt the paradigm to fit their belief systems. They will cram their belief system into another model that does not conform to scientific reality. For example, the Creation Museum in Kentucky is an excellent example of what I call: *Paradigm Cramming*. If science doesn't cooperate with the literal interpretation of Genesis, then: *We'll be sure to fit our belief model so that it will conform to it. Puff! Done! It's just like Genesis says. Alleluia!* I ask, - really? - Not so fast fellas! In my opinion, the evolution of our species is only as natural a process and is part and parcel of the self-organizing Intelligence of the Universe which just IS. Science is part of that process and is observable and measurable. Science and Source are part of the whole and the unity of all things within that whole.

When people refuse to let go of their paradigms or consider new models, this leads to an unfortunate condition, according to Joel Barker, known as *Paradigm Paralysis*. It is another example of Polarization (as in Opposite Strengths) or stuckness. *My paradigm is the ONLY paradigm; My view of the world is the correct view, and no other opinion is acceptable,* etc. When people get stuck they suffer the same conditions we saw in the polarization process; they don't advance in their learning and development, and they do not improve as spiritual beings. They are rigid and inflexible. *My way is the only way,* is their refrain. *My belief is the only real belief.* One of my best friends, Gerald, has threatened so many times to have a bumper sticker printed which says: *My Jesus can beat the crap out of your Jesus!* To me, that is brilliance! It clearly illustrates the variety of interpretations by the so-called followers, of who this figure named Jesus really stood for. I think that would turn a lot of polarized heads.

In 1995, I was assigned to work in Slovakia just 6 years after the communist regime toppled in tandem with the fall of the Soviet Union. In 1993, Slovakia obtained its Independence from the Czech Republic. As an emerging nation, the United States, through the U.S. Agency for International Development (USAID), responded to the newly formed Slovakian government's request for help with their growing epidemic of alcohol and other drugs of abuse.

I worked twice with the Slovakians. The first group was comprised primarily of teachers and principals in Bratislava. That was difficult training. My co-trainer and I noticed that the participants were reticent to open up and be honest about the conditions of alcohol and other drug abuse in their schools. They were non-participatory, and that worried us. One can't have training if the trainees can't demonstrate what they have learned and been able to shift their paradigms. After a long meeting with the individual assigned by the Slovakian authorities to coordinate the logistics of the training, we knew that the problem was not with the school personnel, but with this particular individual who was very suspicious of *these Imperialist Americans*. He was still touting the communist party line, even though the communist party was not running the country. He was challenging and uncooperative. He looked at us with disdain and contempt. After all, we were the enemy. We did everything in our power to win him over and explain to him that we were there to help the country and not take it over.

Realizing that the Slovakian government official was not going to budge on his stand, we concentrated our efforts on the participants and ignored the official as best we could. I took the group through the Opposite Strengths Program. That was the first break-through we were able to accomplish as they discovered how Polarization had dominated their culture and their behaviors as a result. We tied in that process with the whole Paradigm presentation, and they ultimately turned around. They produced viable and implementable action plans for their schools and communities, and they developed a culture of inclusiveness as opposed to exclusiveness when it came to student life and student awareness of social issues, such as substance abuse. Their plans were so doable, implementable and complete that the Slovakian official could not hold back any longer. He capitulated by praising the participants publicly for their excellent work and apologized to us privately for his recalcitrance.

Cults, cultish belief systems, churches and societal groups (especially the radicals at either end of the spectrum) have devised a critical recruitment technique that I call: *Paradigm Hooking*. A Paradigm Hook is a subset of thoughts that are derived from the main body of paradigms of the belief system. These subsets trap people into the belief system by guilt, fear, or by making unrealistic and absurd promises or guaranteeing special status with a deity or whatever else imaginable that the belief system is selling. For example, I heard these phrases many times in my own recruitment process: *You are here because the "divine beings" guided you here. Only a select few are guided to come to us. Therefore, you must have an extraordinary divine mission that only you can fulfill.* This is what I call the *you-are-so-very-special-paradigm hook,* and the ego feeds readily on that one. Then, once you're recruited, that usually is succeeded by the *fear/guilt Paradigm Hook:* which states: *If you leave us then you will incur a grave sin or karma, and therefore you will spend centuries repairing the damage that you've done to your soul and to mankind."*

The more involved I got into the cult, the more dangerous any consideration of abandoning the organization became. I even heard the absurd and idiotic idea that *if you leave, you're going to be condemned by the divine powers of the universe and your soul will be destroyed.*

As a Cognitive-Behavioral Counselor, I worked with high-risk offenders in the Criminal Justice system. The nucleus of my work centered on the following principle: If you are able to change the thinking of the offender, you most likely will change the ensuing behavior that that thinking promotes. In other words, change the mentality, change the behavior. To quote Lao-Tzu from 2500 BC: *"Change your Thoughts, Change your Life."* The Cognitive-Behavioral Model looks like this: (1). A Situation presents itself; (2). A value or interpretation is assigned to it by our mind: good, dangerous, horrible, threatening, menacing, etc.; (3). Additional thoughts are generated about the value or interpretation given to the situation. For example: *If I don't do this I will suffer, the circumstances are out of control, and I need to find a way to control it, He, she, it, is out to get me, etc.* (4). Feelings are generated from the previous interpretation of the situation and the ensuing thoughts that were produced as a result. Those feelings could be anger, fear, anxiety, happiness, elation, joy, trepidation, loathing, etc. The next step in the model is: (5). Behaviors. As a result of the interpretations or perceptions of the situation, the ensuing thoughts and feelings, one is prone to take action. These translate into behaviors: beating someone up, robbing them of food, cursing at someone, freezing in a panic and taking no action (which is a behavior in and of itself). And finally (6). Outcomes: the person was arrested, he/she was given an award, one regrets the negative behaviors, etc.

Having this thinking cycle available to me would, in my opinion, have helped me realize more quickly that the toxic beliefs I was exposed to and their ensuing feelings were not in my highest and best interest. I would've recognized the poison more readily. But when you are steeped in the belief system, you are hypnotized into believing these absurdities, and then you get trapped into many man-made dilemmas that are about as real as ice-cream cones in non-existent hell. So, the traumas became multiple and stacked. They created a barrage of emotions such as guilt, fear, confusion, anger, entrapment, anxiety, panic, depression, self-doubt and self-condemnation among many others. I lost my self-identity. I was a walking robot, confused and wholly manipulated like a puppet on a string of lies in a barren intellectual, emotional and spiritual wasteland.

When all was said and done, and when I was at the very bottom of the seemingly bottomless pit of sadness and depression, I said to myself: *God would want me to be a productive human being.* <u>*I know that to be an absolute truth.*</u> *God would want me to help other people.* <u>*I know that also to be a total truth.*</u> *But I can do none of these things when I am so incapacitated by the way I am acting and feeling,* <u>*I know this also to be an absolute truth.*</u> *So, therefore, I reject and abandon all of these thoughts and ideas that are making me feel this way. I refuse the TG and all of the lieutenants and sub-lieutenants and their teachings because* <u>*I know that, that for me right now, at this time and place it is the right thing for me to do.*</u> *Therefore, I will obey my Higher Authority, and I will abandon this snake pit and all of its venom.* When I came to these conclusions, I knew that I was finally free to leave and forsake it forever. In spite of its apparent simplicity, I knew that this was a profound truth and I instinctively knew that it was inspired by that Higher Authority. I know in my heart that that is true for me to this very day. I am convinced that Jesus knew how talented the false ones could tender their nets of deceit and how difficult it could be to extricate oneself from them. Thus, His statement: *"By their fruits, ye shall know them."* (Mathew 7:20). So, I deduct from this that He was saying: *You won't know on your own the snares these individuals have so maliciously thrown at you. The only way you will know is by the feelings and emotions that arise from being in contact with their energies and their ideas.*

CHAPTER 19

UNDERSTANDING THE NEUROPHYSIOLOGY AND THE HYPNOTIC EFFECT OF BELIEFS

"Beliefs have the power to create and the power to destroy. Human beings have the awesome ability to take any experience of their lives and create a meaning that disempowers them or one that can literally save their lives."
~ Tony Robbins

NEUROPHYSIOLOGY OF BRAINWAVES

One of the most sinister aspects of the addiction to toxic belief systems, and more specifically cultish practices is the mood-altering and hypnotizing effects these can have on unsuspecting participants. In a way, any belief system can become a drug. The process is simple: you get polarized on any one of your core strengths, especially, non-evidence based Theoretical Thinking, and the wolves in sheep's clothing are there to feast upon your persona, your resources, and upon your energy.

Cults in general, cultivate and apply mind or conscience altering methods, such as chanting, light and sound hyper-entrainment, repetitive body motions, drumming, sex, etc. The primary objective of these practices is to create a deep-seated hypnotic effect with which to encode their beliefs and ideas profoundly into the person's psyche. These techniques prepare the subconscious mind to be accepting of a fear-based conglomerate of malware of the most destructive kind, which is then profoundly anchored within the conscious, and more importantly the subconscious mind. If we can use computer terms, this acts as a platform for an operating system that is designed to mold thought, beliefs, and consequently, behaviors, to hold the person hostage in an observably enslaved state of being.

There are many ways that people can become polarized. First, they have a tendency to get polarized due to their innate nature, or based on their predominant personal or emotional issues. And secondly, they may get stuck due to the conscious and/or subconscious exposure to false or detrimental concepts while in an altered state of consciousness (ASC). This modified state as defined by Arnold Ludwig, (also called altered state of mind or mind alteration), is any condition which is significantly different from a typical waking beta wave state. Many of these ASC's occur when the senses are stimulated in a way that profoundly involves the neuronal mechanism that affects the hypnotic state of consciousness or what is referred to as the hypnogogic state.

These practices can be seen in traditional religions or in non-traditional belief platforms, such as specific shamanic practices. As mentioned before, these include chanting, drumming, dancing, singing, wailing, posturing, thrashing, speaking in tongues, fasting, etc., and of course taking mind-altering hallucinogens such as, ayahuasca, peyote or mushrooms which will change the mind-state to an altered reality. The more senses that are involved in the process, the more profound the hypnogogic trance state will tend to be. This would also include smells (incenses, essential oils, etc.) or physical stimulation such as massaging, specific body part stimulations, sex, etc.

In the early 1990's I discovered a revolutionary form of therapy called EEG Neurofeedback or EEG Biofeedback. Neurofeedback is an evidence-based form of treatment that trains the states of arousal in the brain by increasing the brain waves that will promote balance and inhibit those which cause instability or abnormalities in mind-states of attention, mood, and behaviors. After a lengthy training and certification process, I became certified to practice EEG Neurofeedback. The excellent training I received prepared me to practice as a Neurotherapist for 15 years, not just as a Practioner, but as well as a trainer for professionals. These included training psychologists and psychiatrists, not only in the United States but in Europe and Latin America.

Neurofeedback works by measuring brainwaves (which are associated with different states of arousal) and rewarding and/or inhibiting specific brain waves to obtain a balance in attention, emotional and mental stability, and to inhibit instabilities associated with emotional or mental disorders.

What are Brainwaves? The brain's 100 billion neurons or brain cells (called neurons), are continually chatting and communicating with each other and they use electricity and chemistry to accomplish that. The chemistry part of the equation is identified as a neurotransmitter. The principal ones are classified as Serotonin, Dopamine, Noradrenaline, GABA, etc. Scientists have identified approximately 60 neurotransmitters. The combination of millions of neurons sending signals at once produces an enormous amount of electrical activity in the brain, which can be detected using sensitive medical equipment (such as an EEG), measuring electricity levels over diverse areas of the scalp.

This is accomplished through a complex array of computers and

EEG amplifiers. But Neurofeedback works just as well for fine tuning the brain to increase optimal or peak performance.

The brainwaves are divided into the following:

Delta: 0.5 – 3.9 Hz.
Theta: 4 – 7 Hz.
Alpha: 8- 11 Hz
Low Beta (Sensory Motor Rhythms or SMR) 12-15 Hz.
Beta – 18-22 Hz.
High Beta 22-30 Hz.
Gamma – 30 and above.

Delta is the slowest brainwave and is registered when we are in deep, dreamless sleep. Theta is referred to as the *hypnogogic state* because it is in this frequency that we dream. This is also the frequency that is used to induce a state of high suggestibility or is referred to as the gateway to the hypnotic state. Theta is also the path to the sub-conscious mind. If you want to program your subconscious mind with a behavior/attitude or a command for future performance, you must do so primarily in Theta. This 4-7 Hertz frequency is the state that is reached when a therapist wishes to access information during a Hypnotherapy session. This is important for you to remember because it will relate to the last section of this book on PLR (hypnotic regression) and other forms of hypnotherapy as conducted by Dr. Michael Newton, Dr. Brian Weiss and other hypnotherapists all over the world.

Alpha is the meditation brainwave. It is in this state that we are able to calm our mind and body and experience a deep state of relaxation. Even though in Delta we are in an unconscious state, in Theta we are in a semi-conscious state. In Alpha, we are conscious but deeply relaxed with eyes closed. Low Beta through Gamma denotes high states of conscious awareness and attention, and we primarily produce these brain waves with eyes open and increasing levels of concentration and focus. The Lower frequencies (Delta – Alpha) are also classified as representing states of *under-arousal* whereas High Beta thru Gamma represents states of *over-arousal*. Disorders such as depression (clinical or otherwise); ADD (attention deficit disorder), or ADHD (attention deficit hyperactive disorder); some anxiety disorders, etc., would fall under the category of *under-arousal*. On the other hand, *over-arousal* would signify states of high stress, anger, raging, the fight/flight response, etc.

Neurofeedback is an evidence-based practice which means that it is research-based and has a long track record of clinical trials and is scientifically well documented. The process is a highly effective one and is used to deal with anything from closed head injuries (with promising results) to bruxism. The procedure uses a series of computers to retrain the brain to inhibit the unbalanced brain waves and reward or reinforce the balancing brain waves to create the desirable mental and emotional states. Please see the appendix for more information. I am sharing this process with you to give you another essential resource for a drug-free alternative to help alleviate anxiety or depression.

The other reason is to shed light on how some cultist environments manipulate the brainwaves to create a high degree hypnogogic stimulation. This, in essence, opens the back door to the subconscious, thus making it easier to implant cultist sound bites. I believe this is what happened to me. We were forced to chant for long periods of time (induced theta evoked potentials) and then have us listen to the deranged leader as transmitted the false narratives from the so-called divine ones. This jibber-jabber was nothing more than regurgitated conscious and subconscious garbage, often disguised as so-called profound teachings from the cosmos. Most of the time, this harangue was composed of nonsensical concepts utterly devoid of meaning and reason, but we were advised that we had to remember the information or experience much disfavor from the imagined divine ones, resulting in harsh punishments for us.

The most critical reason for understanding the underhanded and sinister methods of the cultists (and many religions), is knowing the mechanism of the brain that primarily cements the toxic data in our psyche. Once you reverse the process, you can unlock and disarm all of the conscious and unconscious ticking time bombs. This is accomplished in the practice of clinical applications of hypnotherapy and regression.

As part of my certification process, I had to submit to at least 30 to 50 Neurofeedback sessions to help me undergo the fine tuning of my brain and learn how this process could impact me and consequently how it impacts other clients. After approximately 10 sessions I noticed that I was calmer, I slept much more soundly, I could concentrate for lengthier time periods than before, and I developed a sense of peace, never experienced since I joined the cult. These brain states originated out of the sessions that we call *high frequency* or eyes open. The significant changes for me came when I switched to *low-frequency* Neurofeedback sessions or eyes closed. These are called Alpha/Theta sessions. They are designed to reward Alpha brain waves (8-11 Hz.) and eventually Theta brain waves (4-7 Hz.) or the hypnogogic brain states that were mentioned previously. The Alpha/Theta sessions helped to anchor a state of complete peace, and I experienced profound healing at an intense level. It helped me to have a sense of connectedness to all things and to feel wholeness in a field of profound spiritual oneness. This state is hard to describe, but the bottom line is that the sense of time is lost and we don't want it to end because it promotes a profound sense of peace.

Occasionally, a client will experience what is called a *cross-over*. That happens when Alpha drops abruptly, and Theta shoots up dramatically. That signals that the brain has entered a hypnogogic state and visual stimulation or imagery is experienced as in a REM (rapid eye movement) state. As a general rule, it is a very healing state that occurs at profound levels of the psyche. I had numerous cross-overs, and all of them came with a message disguised as a visual metaphor. My conscious mind could not make sense out of them, but my subconscious mind did as it brought on an incredibly broad understanding or clarification and closure of internal emotional conflicts. It felt like my inner struggles had suddenly been resolved. I experienced profound changes without noticing how they happened. I was calmer, more centered. The memories of the dark past no longer had the emotional charge they once had. I could navigate through most of those memories without emotional repercussions. I don't think that my recovery could have been complete without Neurofeedback.

Cross-overs do occur, but more as an exception than the rule, at least that has been my experience as a Neurotherapist. However, occasionally, the cross-over can reach highly intense levels of sensory awareness that spills over into a profoundly altered state of consciousness. These translate in many cases into amazing spiritual experiences rich in hypnogogic imagery and symbolism. These events can be profoundly transformative and cause an unexpected *spiritual emergence* to take place.

On one occasion, I was working with a middle-aged recovering poly-substance abuser. I'll call him Larry. His primary drug of choice was alcohol, but at the height of his addiction, he used other drugs, namely barbiturates to reinforce the alcohol and stimulants afterward to arouse him and help him be more awake. He had successfully completed in-patient detox and 30 days of in-patient treatment in a certified alcohol and drug abuse facility and had at least 5 years sobriety with diligent participation in a local 12-step program. Typically, our protocols call for at least 30 high-frequency (eyes open) Beta-SMR (sensory-motor rhythm) sessions. These sessions help the brain reach a level of homeostasis which results in more mental, and emotional stability, accompanied by an increased ability to concentrate and maintain a single-focused state of attention. In other words, it helps clients be more in control of their emotions and be able to pay much better attention. Thus, if the client had ADD (Attention Deficit Disorder) or ADHD (Attention Deficit Hyperactivity Disorder), the symptoms of these disorders would be reduced significantly. These advances were measured by performance variables and other visual tests such as the T.O.V.A. (Test of Variables of Attention) which is an FDA cleared continuous performance test (CPT). These changes occurred all without the use of any ADD/ADHD medication.

Larry completed his 30 eyes open sessions, and he was ready for his eyes closed sessions, again called Alpha/Theta sessions. Previous to his Neurofeedback sessions, Larry had experienced frequent bouts of anger and impulsivity. That is what is commonly known among recovering alcoholics as a *dry drunk*. These symptoms were significantly reduced with the open eyes sessions, but he still experienced periodic episodes of raging and explosive melt-downs. These events were triggered by normal stressors, such as traffic, conflicts with other individuals, poor performance in sports (primarily golf), and conflicts with his young wife and child.

We began his Alpha/Theta sessions, and his raging was reduced even further. He was calmer and more composed, especially when he was challenged by stressful environmental factors, mentioned previously. He only experienced one or two shallow cross-overs with some imagery, but nothing remarkable. On his 10th session of Alpha/Theta, however, he had a very significant cross-over. His Theta (4-7 Hz) shot up way above the normal range, and his Alpha (8-11 Hz) dropped markedly. At one point, I observed an exceptional increase in REM (Rapid Eye Movements) which is characteristic of the dream state. Then suddenly, his brainwaves flattened out to a range of between 2 and 3 Hz. His breathing, although steady, was very faint. He was in this state for approximately 5 to 10 minutes receiving Theta auditory feedback, which in our system sounded like Tibetan gongs with ocean waves as a background sound effect. My clinical assistant and I were in awe of such unusual brainwave signatures.

At 10 minutes in this state, I decided to slowly bring him out of the profound state of consciousness that he was in by decreasing his Theta thresholds and increasing more Alpha (8-11 Hz) activity. This was heard as a pinging sound with the sound of a running brook as a background soundtrack. His Alpha slowly increased, and he began to emerge from that deep state. It took us about 30 minutes to bring him back to full conscious awareness. When he opened his glassy eyes with a far-away look, he said: *Where did you take me? I loved every minute of it! I was in a place of total peace and love like I had never experienced before. At one point, I started to go through a darkened tunnel and then, like coming up from a deep well, I saw the faces of deceased loved ones who were peering over the edge of the well, and I could hear them say: Oh look who's coming!* I asked him if at any time he felt fear, and he said: *I never felt fear, on the contrary, I felt unconditional love. I was aware that I was part of everything and the whole Universe was a part of me. I also knew that I had a guide close by, but I never saw his face, but I knew he was guiding me and I was safe with him. His loving energy was almost overwhelming.* He continued: *I heard my loved ones say to me that it wasn't my turn yet and I had to return. Surprisingly, I knew they spoke the truth.* On the other hand, he also reported hearing other parts of his consciousness say: *I hope these guys know how to bring me back!*

We conducted a 15-minute eyes-open session. This helped Larry to become more alert and anchored. When we got him up and out of the therapy chair, we took him outside into a garden to get fresh air and to help him get more present. Larry repeatedly said: *Oh wow! Listen to the bird's sing! Look how green the grass is and how beautiful the flowers are.* He was still in an altered state of consciousness, and we felt that for his own safety it wasn't wise for him to drive home, so we made arrangements to get him back safely. We consulted with the clinical director of our parent company that trained us and kept her updated-on Larry's progress or lack thereof. She recommended specific stabilizing protocols which helped Larry in his stride toward a more significant stabilization.

Before Larry arrived home, we called his wife and told him about his experience and to expect him to be less present than usual. We reassured her that he would eventually settle down to his usual old self. She subsequently reported that he was very mellow and almost euphoric, and he was very loving toward her and their small child. To our amazement, she said that that same evening she was suffering from a rather intense migraine and told Larry that she was in quite a bit of pain and was about to take her migraine pain medication. She said he instinctively reached over and touched her head. She reported that almost within seconds of physically making contact with her, the migraine subsided significantly to the point where she had no need for painkillers. She also remarked that she could feel the energy pouring out of his hands.

We continued to work with Larry, and we administered about twenty eyes open sessions. It took him about five full sittings to finally get his footing back and be able to walk the straight line, so to speak. The long-term effects of Larry's experience resulted in a calmer and more centered person. He was genuinely interested in replicating his transcendent experiences by practicing daily meditation. He was often disappointed by his inability to fully re-experience his previous euphoric episodes. His interest in subject matters of a spiritual nature was awakened, and he read more books on spirituality than ever before. He was remarkably more amiable and less prone to unexpected outbursts.

This extraordinary adventure I was able to witness as a practicing Neurotherapist was my first exposure to almost the same characteristics of Near Death Experiences (NDE's) and other unusual phenomena addressed later in this book. My experiences with Larry would resound once again, years later, as I dove into the after-life research that clarified so many spiritual enigmas and helped me to at last find a resolution to the traumas of the past. Larry was, in effect, my first teacher in this vibrant area of pioneering research.

Finally, I would like to take this opportunity to address the work of the Dr. Michael Newton Institute that I describe later in this book. All of these hypnotherapeutic modalities could possibly be more efficiently facilitated in much less time than currently is taking place by using Neurotherapy. The audio/visual technology now exists to make this a reality. I pose this as a possible research project that may prove very rewarding and open brand-new avenues and protocols to make Hypnotherapeutic regressions less taxing and less time-consuming. I would venture to say also that the profound Theta states achieved by Neurotherapy could lead to even more profound revelations by clients in hypnotherapy.

Neurofeedback is currently used in many clinical settings, from alcohol and drug abuse treatment centers to peak performance clinics for professionals and athletes. It is an excellent way to treat ADD/ADHD, behavioral problems and emotional instabilities with substantial evidential results, and in most cases without the use of other drugs.

If you are currently having problems with anxiety or depression or any other symptoms, whether cult created or not, you may want to seriously look into the drug-free therapeutic benefits of Neurofeedback.

CHAPTER 20

TRANSPERSONAL EXPERIENCES

"The day science begins to study non-physical phenomena, it will make more progress in one decade than in all the previous centuries of its existence."
~ Nikola Tesla

In July 1986, my mother was very ill and hospitalized in an Intensive Care Unit. She had been there three weeks and did not seem to be improving, on the contrary, she seemed to be slipping more and more into unconsciousness. In the early morning of the Thursday of the 3rd week, I had a vivid dream in full color. It was one of those types of nighttime visions that if it had a label, it would say: *You better pay real close attention to this dream.* And I did.

In my dream, I was sitting on the side of a dirt road. In the distance, I saw a team of horses galloping at full speed creating a dust storm that hid a fast-approaching vehicle that they pulled. Suddenly, and without warning the horses came to an abrupt stop right in front of me, obscured by a great cloud of dust which eventually settled. There sat a Wells Fargo type stagecoach. Curiously, the coach had no drivers, just the agitated team of six horses. Finally, when everything settled down, I noticed a woman sitting in the back seat of the coach looking at me from the right back window. At first, I didn't recognize who the woman was. She was very elegantly dressed in an impressive hat with feathers and what appeared to be a ruffled silk dress. Her makeup was exquisite, and she had an otherworldly glow about her. She had a huge smile on her face.

As I focused more closely, I saw that it was my mom. I felt like yelling out to her: *Mom! What are you doing in that thing?* But I held my breath instead. She appeared to be very happy. Then she leaned her head a bit more out of the window and said to me in a pleasant, melodious voice and without moving her lips: *Patrick, I am pleased because I'm going home!* Then, without mentioning anything else, she transmitted a telepathic message: *I love you.* In the background, I could hear the song "Going to take a Sentimental Journey." At that point, the stagecoach wheels blurred to the fierce gallop of the horses and my mom waved her hand good-bye with a big smile on her glowing face. The stagecoach disappeared in a cloud of dust as I fought back the tears.

The next morning, I was driving my sisters to the hospital and unbelievably "Going to Take a Sentimental Journey" came over the radio. Awe-struck, I held back the tears as the dream came back into my conscious awareness and in full color. I knew then that the end of my mom's earthly journey was apparently in sight. Her departure message was all her doing. I suspect she planned it that way. If she was going to go out, it was going to be in full style! But what was up with the stagecoach? That threw me. I still haven't been able to figure that one out unless she was referring to a past life that held particular significance for her. She was an exquisite and striking woman who appreciated beautiful things. She sold makeup for a living, at least part-time. She would never dream of leaving the house in a state of disarray or without her makeup impeccably applied to highlight her beautiful features and deep hazel eyes. She was also very much the sentimental type who would cry at the drop of a handkerchief, especially if it had to do with a love affair gone wrong or the lover who vanished leaving the maiden broken-hearted.

We arrived at the hospital, and we held a closed family meeting to discuss whether mom should be moved to hospice care or something else. My sister said that she was going to talk to my unconscious mother and tell her that everyone is okay and that it was acceptable for her to move on. That was at 10 am. Shortly afterward, my sister went into her room and whispered in her ear that everyone is taken care of and that if it was her time to move on, that she could, and no one was holding her back. At 3 pm, she left us for her heavenly abode.

I never had another dream like that until one morning in 2009. It was early, perhaps 5:30 or 6 am. I thought it was a dream, but it turned out to be more than that. The experience is one that, until now, I have told to only 2 or 3 of my closest friends who know about those type of transpersonal events and have experienced them, themselves. My hesitation to relate this to others outside of my tight circle of friends was a fear that I would be doubted and labeled, perhaps, as crazy or mentally imbalanced. Admittedly, I thought I would be mocked and made fun of. So, until now, I have kept the event to myself. So, this is my real mystical *coming-out*, if you will.

On this particular morning, I was awakened by a series of almost euphoric, very intense feelings of love and peace. These sensations were unlike anything I had ever experience in my life. The absolute peace and profound love I felt was beyond any earthly understanding, and my mind struggled to find words to adequately, even come close to describing it. In my vision (or dream), a very luminous Being appeared before me and emanated intense unconditional love, compassion, and understanding. I had the feeling that this Being was not unfamiliar to me, but I had no reference point to positively identify him.

I had a sense that I knew him, but I could not place him for the life of me. He had light brown hair, bordering on blond and exquisitely hypnotizing eyes. The color of his eyes was of a violet-blue hue, a color that was not of this world. And, again, the peace and unconditional love that I felt radiating from this luminous Being were beyond my limited human vocabulary. I couldn't possibly even come close to describing the experience. It practically sent me into a semi-conscious state of ecstasy, I was on the brink of tears of incomprehensible joy and comfort. Once again, I felt like I already knew him and that we were very close, but I couldn't remember where and how we were connected.

The scene of the experience took place in a hallway at work. It was at that time when I was about to undergo a very positive professional change. I was to be promoted to a position of counseling high-risk offenders in a criminal justice setting. The luminous Being stood on my left and slightly behind me, and telepathed me: *Look at that man standing there.* I looked to my right, and I saw a middle-aged man with dark-rimmed glasses. He looked confused and dull. The Master said to me: *Go and take his hands.* I hesitated. I didn't know this man. Why would I take his hands? I thought to myself. The Master said again with more emphasis: *Go ahead Patrick, don't be afraid, take his hands.* I approached the man, and I could smell alcohol on his breath. Hesitantly, I took his hands, and the Master said: *Go and heal him from his alcoholism and help all those that you can.* He continued with a profound telepathic message: *These are rare opportunities given to you to help you advance quickly in your earthly mission. Take full advantage of it as we are all cheering for your complete success in this noble endeavor.*

The experience ended as quickly as it began. That was the end of the most intense sacred experience I have ever had. I awoke from the dream if that's what it was. Dazed and confused, I was overcome with emotion and with peace so intense that I feared moving or getting up from my bed should it break the spell. So, I remained as still as possible. With my eyes closed, I reflected on what just had happened and felt comforted entirely to the core of my being. The peace and unconditional love that emanated from my luminous visitor continued to saturate every molecule and atom of my entire person, body, soul, mind, and feelings.

That day at work was extraordinary. I was unusually calm and peaceful. I purposely walked to the spot in my building where the scene of my experience had unfolded. I stood precisely at the spot where the vision had taken place, and I relived the incredible experience all over again, but without re-experiencing the intense feelings of peace and love. I just couldn't get it out of my thoughts. I used the memories of that experience to satisfy and enrich my spiritual longing for resolution and more importantly, to know that I was being helped from the *other side*. I still feel intensely connected to my friend from that ethereal dimension.

I share this experience with you my reader because I don't believe I was special or had to have any spiritual prerequisite to have had that experience. Anybody who has embarked on a spiritual journey can have these types of experiences. And if you have an experience of this type, receive it as a gift from Spirit.

It was after that episode that I began the new phase of my professional life. As mentioned before, I conducted cognitive behavioral groups for high-risk men and women on probation. I know I was particularly called to do this work. I found myself developing a singular passion for teaching these criminal offenders. I found out later many of them were significantly impacted by the group experiences. Their ways of thinking and feeling and their lives, in general, were changed for the better. It turned into a sacred work for me. You can't teach anyone an important subject and not expect to impact their lives in one form or another, either in small ways or significant ones.

I worked 8 years conducting cognitive behavioral groups for high-risk offenders in a criminal justice setting. I was enjoying my job and working well with my assigned students. It was shortly after completing my 8th year on the project that I experienced a few episodes of unexpected health challenges that brought up a lot of fear and anxiety. I practiced meditation and diligently applied Byron Katie's, The Work. I used Emotional Freedom Technique and other healing modalities, including energy work. After an intense period of self-work, I achieved a sense of stability and a return to normalcy. But the most important breakthrough for me was questioning the assumptions I was making that were, in the end, leading me to believe an endless list of lies that provoked unwarranted fears. I could almost hear my rational mind saying to me: "Got you again!".

However, the nagging questions that had been at the back of my mind, since the early years of my life were still there, and the same questions that lead me to explore the cult. And I suppose, in many respects, these are the same questions or similar ones that we all have as humans. In retrospect, and considering that I had never resolved them, I believe these were at the source of most of my sensitivity to stress and fear. Those questions, were: Why am I here? What is my mission in this life? What happens to us after we die? Is there really hell? Why the fear? Why the anxiety? Is there a devil? Is God all-loving? Where is the justice in this unjust world? Why did I grow up in such a dysfunctional family? Why did I join the cult? Will I be judged and condemned when this life is over? The list went on.

I felt a compelling need to get some answers. So, I searched and searched for answers, and I asked my Higher Power for help in getting answers that were not forthcoming and had been so elusive and pervasively out of reach. When it came to reading books, I was more attracted to scientific ones that provided spiritual reflections or had an interconnection. Many times, I would read just scientific books written for the layperson. I was very hesitant to venture too far from my comfort zone. The first of those books was the _Tao of Physics_ by Fritjof Capra. I loved that book, and it helped me to flex to my practical *what is thinking* (referring back to the Opposite Strengths program) as opposed to the non-evidenced based theoretical thinking strength of *what-could-be-thinking*. I will make reference to it later. After that, I read other physics-type books that helped me see a clear connection between science and spirituality such as the _Dancing Wu Li Masters: An Overview of the New Physics_ by Gary Zukav. All of these books had a profound effect on me.

I took up reading the _Tao Te Ching_ (translation by Stephen Mitchell), and that provided a new worldview of the interconnectedness of all things in the Universe. I learned that Chi, the energy of the Universe is everywhere and flows through all things. I learned that emptiness is so revered by the Taoists because it promotes the silence of contemplation in meditation. Alan Watt's: <u>*Tao, the Watercourse Way*</u> was also an exceptional read for me. It also reinforced the oneness of all things in the Universe, and that the duality of *God vs. the devil* was very much a Western concept not embraced by Eastern philosophy and culture. I would later learn that, like the Yin and the Yang, duality explains the core of our lessons and the experiences that duality brings into our experiential awareness to help our souls learn and grow. This was made more evident to me when I read about the metaphor that if we evolved exclusively in a white world, where everything was white and only white, we would assume that everything in the Universe was white. But it's not until shades of darker colors other than white come into our worldview that helps us to understand the nature of white and appreciate white for its own innate nature. This occurs only when we see the comparison in the quality of duality. This could be compared to light vs. dark or higher vibrational patterns as opposed to lower vibrational patterns. I prefer the former.

CHAPTER 21

CLIMBING OUT ON MY OWN LIMB

"Many times, what we perceive as an error or
failure is actually a gift. And eventually, we
find that lessons learned from that discouraging
experience prove to be of great worth."
~ Richelle E. Goodrich

"By seeking and blundering, we learn."
~ Johann Wolfgang von Goethe

It was vital for me to learn from my past mistakes and adhere to the well-tested road of evidential theory and practical application, no matter what the subject. Venturing into *New Age* genre of writings was very uncomfortable for me. I was not going to make the same mistake again as I did with the cult.

In that light, I set the following parameters for myself in exploring new material, especially transpersonal/spiritual type information. Those parameters were as follows:

1. It had to be evidential or based on research that ruled out speculation, and it had to be statistically significant.
2. It had to conform to the non-reptilian brain principle rule. (Non-fear based). If the teaching or information causes fear, its source most likely is the Limbic System (the amygdala) or the reptilian brain and should be rejected.
3. I created and adhered to the following formula: F=L+I+E+D=D: Fear=Lies+Inaccuracies+Ego+Deceptions=Discard.
4. It had to have its philosophical and practical base firmly anchored in scientific knowledge and tested by scientific methods of research as much as possible.
5. The information had to serve mankind's advancement mentally, emotionally, and especially, spiritually.

After many, many years of trekking in the desert, of spiritual austerity, so to speak, I embarked on a judiciously orchestrated reading adventure. My choice of books or subject matters were cautiously selected according to the guidelines I set for myself. My reading journey seemed to be a progressive one. It appeared to have been meticulously and deliberately planned, but apparently, not by me. My exploratory trips into the afterlife research were as if an invisible hand was guiding me.

Books flowed from one genre into another. The initial books were strictly on scientific themes, mainly physics, to a unique marriage between science and spirituality. Two of those authors and books that stood out for me was, as previously mentioned, Fritjof Capra's <u>*The Tao of Physics.*</u> The other one was Dr. Amit Goswami's <u>*Physics of the Soul.*</u> My understanding of how science and spirituality are genuinely one became more and more apparent to me as levels of vibrational frequencies intersecting at different levels of quantum activity in layered sets of dimensions of energy and information within a unified field of all possibilities. This added up to a tiny little picture of what real quantum spirituality might remotely look like. Instinctively, I knew that all this was impossible to describe and that's what contributed to my ever-present search for answers to the mystery of life and the afterlife. But my questions to life's fundamental questions persisted and seemed to demand an explanation. Why am I here? What is the purpose of my life? If I have a mission what is that mission? What happens to us after we die? Etc.

In late 2014, I was searching on Amazon for more books on the subject, and keeping in step with the previous sequential pattern (which I firmly believe was orchestrated from a Higher Level), I was led to Dr. Michael Newton's *Journey of Souls* and *Destiny of Souls*. It seemed like my Amazon webpage describing *Journey of Souls* was frozen. I attempted to fast forward to the next screen, but it would not budge. I thought that was odd. So, I stayed on the page. I pressed the "look inside" tab above the book, and the page *magically unfroze* itself. I read as much as I could. It was then that I realized these books conformed to all of the parameters that I had set for myself. I took the risk to explore further. I read the reviews, and I was virtually awe-stricken with the contents! A still small voice in my mind said to me: *You must read these books.*

The research of the late Dr. Michael Newton had the most profound effect on me. (He passed away on September 21st, 2016). Dr. Newton was a Clinical Psychotherapist and Clinical Hypnotherapist. Dr. Newton began his practice in 1956, and he considered himself a traditional Psychotherapist/Hypnotherapist. Reincarnation was in no way part of his glossary, psychological or otherwise. He used hypnosis to try to uncover the origins of childhood emotional and physical trauma. He did not consider himself religious. As a matter of fact, quite the contrary, he was not really a believer in a deity or an afterlife. In simple terms, he was an atheist. But as we will see, that soon would change.

The books *Journey of Souls* and *Destiny of Souls* described incredible breakthroughs in the field of hypnotherapy and more specifically about past life regression, a theme that Dr. Newton initially rejected with a passion as *New Agey*. Subsequently, Dr. Newton wrote *Memories of the Afterlife and Life Between Lives, Hypnotherapy for Spiritual Regression*. So, having a background in Psychology, and with all my clinical experience in Neurotherapy, these books very much facilitated my exploration into new realms of thought. I'm glad I took that risk. These books would prove to answer so many of my questions and free me at last from the years of the lies of religion and more importantly, of the cult. Additionally, these books contained a wealth of spiritual information and significant spiritual insights and messages. The books resounded deeply for me. My heart told me this is what I could trust and needed to absorb.

To describe how I was so drawn to Dr. Newton's work can only be summarized in two words, credible and evidential. Shortly after he began his practice in 1956, Dr. Newton describes how he got involved in all of this past life regression hypnotherapy. He would tell patients who called asking if he did past life regressions and would politely tell them that he didn't do any of "that New Age stuff." It was in 1956 that the Bridey Murphy case had become so popular. Dr. Newton's office was swamped with calls from people who wanted to know if he did past life regressions. His answer was always the standard one-liner: "Sorry, no I am very traditional. I'm not into 'New Age' thinking." He would politely turn them away. He said in an interview with the filmmaker Rich Martini, "I was very naïve, really."

But then he describes his initiation into the practice of past life regression as one in which he went into it "kicking and screaming." This happened because of a young man who showed up in his office complaining of a pain in his side. Apparently, he had been examined by countless doctors, and none of them could diagnose his condition. Finally, after numerous medical tests, he was told that the pain was psychosomatic and he should go see a psychologist or psychiatrist.

So, Dr. Newton accepted him as a patient and hypnotized him. When he reached a deep theta state (hypnogogic frequency of the brain Chapter 19), he asked the young man many questions about his pain that didn't seem to arrive at any conclusive cause of its origins. This went on for quite a while until he reached a frustrating point in the session and that's when Dr. Newton gave him the command: "Go to the source of your pain." Then suddenly, the young man leaped into the life of a soldier in World War I, when he was a British Sergeant and was being bayoneted. He was in obvious pain and emotionally traumatized. As a general rule, Dr. Newton would immediately desensitize the patient to alleviate his trauma (also known as *abreaction*). Instead, he insisted in asking him questions, like his name, rank, the army unit he was in, the place of his birth and his home, the place where he died in the war, etc. Dr. Newton gathered all of that information and wrote it down. Eventually, after his almost violent abreaction, he desensitized the young man, and he was able to calm him down sufficiently to conclude the session without any residual emotional trauma. The next day, the young man called Dr. Newton thanking him profusely for having cured him. "What do you mean cured?" "Oh yes Dr. Newton, as soon as I left your office the pain in my side completely disappeared!"

Immensely curious, Dr. Newton contacted the British War Office and the Imperial Museum and gave them all of the facts that the young man had given him in the hypnotherapy session. Sure enough, they confirmed the existence of this British Sergeant, his platoon, his hometown, where and how he died in 1916.

Sometime later, a woman came into Dr. Newton's office complaining of depression and not having any friends and unable to establish contact with anyone. He took her into a deep state of hypnosis, and after a long time of inquiring why she was having these feelings and getting nowhere in the session, he finally said to her: "Go to the origin of your loneliness, especially if there's a group of people around you." It seemed that the word *group* was a trigger for her because immediately she brightened up. Dr. Newton mentioned in his instructions to the woman to recall any specific group of friends whom she missed. She immediately started sobbing. When Dr. Newton asked her, what was wrong, she said: "I miss some friends in my group, and that's why I get so lonely on earth." She then happily reported that she saw all of her spiritual family members or as she described them "my soul group." Dr. Newton describes these as the *cluster groups*.

Dr. Newton was curious to know if she was viewing this group in a past life or in the past known as the *in-between lives* period. So, he asked her: "Where are we?" she replied overcome with joy, "Oh, we are in the spirit world! They are right here right now here in your office!" He inquired further why none of them had accompanied her in this life. She said that it was decided in her life planning session, before she came into this life, that the woman needed to do things on her own without relying on her soul group, as she had done in her past lives. When Dr. Newton inquired further, as to why that was that important, she said that she had grown too dependent on them for everything, and she needed to start making decisions on her own and be more self-reliant. It was a lesson that her Higher Self pointed out as being essential for the continued growth of her soul.

Shortly after his experience with these initial cases, Dr. Newton decided to close down his regular psychotherapeutic practice and dedicate the rest of his professional life to giving PLR and LBL sessions. His primary objective was not only to develop a database on the afterlife but to provide individuals the opportunity to heal themselves emotionally or physically in the process.

In 2004 when Dr. Newton's last book *Life Between Lives: Hypnotherapy for Spiritual Regression* was written, it is estimated that about 10,000 regressions had been conducted by Dr. Newton and all of the hypnotherapists from all over the world that he had trained up to that point. Today those numbers far exceed that figure and are estimated at close to 50,000 regressions. What is impressive and which gives evidential support to this information is that all subjects, without exception, have all corroborated basically the same information and have done so consistently across cultural and international boundaries. This fact cannot be ignored. What is the statistical probability of that happening? Virtually none, as any statistician can attest.

Mr. Rich Martini, a Hollywood movie producer, author, and historian has taken a particular interest in Dr. Newton's work and the NDE field. He started out as a skeptic and actually intended to invalidate Dr. Newton's research and the claims derived from Past Lives and Life Between Lives sessions. However, after experiencing several of his own PLR's and LBL's Rich had the first-hand experience of the power of these sessions. He had no further doubts about the validity of the work. He was in awe of the evidential validation that came from Dr. Newton's work. He has four significant books that you might find interesting: *Flipside: A Tourist's Guide on How to Navigate the Afterlife*; *It's a Wonderful Afterlife: Further Adventures in the Flipside Vols. 1 & 2*. And *Hacking the Afterlife: Practical Advice from the Flipside*.

In another case, Rich Martini in his book. *It's A Wonderful Afterlife Vol. I: Further Adventures in the Flipside* (Kindle Page 44; Loc. 836), Mr. Martini describes meeting an Oxford Professor, Robert "B." Mr. "B" remembered a past life in Boston in the 1840's (a city he has never been to in this lifetime but described accurately during his session) and who was married to a woman whom he knows in this lifetime. In his session, he related that the two of them had been living together in Boston. He explained that his wife in that lifetime died prematurely and he became very depressed and died shortly afterward. Rich asked him if he was still friends with this particular woman and he affirmed he was. He asked Mr. "B" not to reveal anything about his session, and, if the woman who he knows in this lifetime was willing, he would arrange for a Newton Institute trained hypnotherapist in New York City, where she lived, to conduct a past life regression. She agreed and had the session in which she revealed precisely the same details of the life which Mr. "B" had reported, including specific facts and circumstances. What are the statistical probabilities of that happening? Again, the answer to that question is none.

After marinating in the work of Dr. Newton, I took up researching the work of Dr. Brian Weiss who has written some significant books on healing and past-life regression. Dr. Weiss, like Dr. Newton, was a traditional therapist, an agnostic, and who did not believe in an afterlife, nor much of anything else related to metaphysics, an afterlife, and much less reincarnation. He firmly adhered to the strict scientific training he received as a psychiatrist, until one day when a patient name Catherine completely changed his life. While under hypnosis, Catherine brought forth descriptions from centuries past in which she lived a prior life. Catherine's hypnotherapy sessions also revealed information about Dr. Weiss' deceased infant son and other evidential information that no one knew, except his wife. She also brought forth deep wisdom from

"Masters" who surrounded her while she was out of her body during her therapy sessions. The information collected from over 4,000 regressions consistently painted the same picture; that an afterlife is a place of infinite and pure unconditional love, where we are not judged and where we go to learn what we could've done better in our lives and how to plan for the eventuality of resolving past mistakes. To quote Dr. Weiss in his book *Same Soul, Many Bodies: Discover the Healing Power of Future Lives Through Progression Therapy*:

"It has taken me twenty-four years to reach the simple truth at the core of this book. We are immortal. We are eternal. Our souls will never die. This being so, we should start acting as if we know that immortality is our blessing. Or to put it more simply, we should prepare for immortality – here, now, today and tomorrow and each day for the rest of our lives."

Dr. Weiss continues: *"How do we prepare? How do immortal people act? In this life, we prepare by learning how to have better relationships; how to be more loving, more compassionate; how to be healthier physically, emotionally, and spiritually; how to help others; how to enjoy this world and yet advance its evolution, advance its healing."* (*Same Soul, Many Bodies*, pg. 17 and 18 Kindle edition).

Following up on the work of Dr. Weiss, I came upon the excellent research by Dr. Jim Tucker of the University of Virginia, Division of Perceptual Studies. His 2 books: *Life Before Life: A Scientific Investigation of Children's Memories of Previous Lives* and his more recent book: *Return to Life: Extraordinary Cases of Children Who Remember Past Lives* describes his research investigating very young children's accounts of memories of past lives. The books are scientifically researched and well documented with highly evidential data to back it up.

One of the best books to summarize all of the significant after-life research is Dr. Mark Pitstick's *Soul Proof: Compelling Evidence You Are an Infinite/Spiritual Energetic Being*. Dr. Pitstick not only rolls out a neat summary of the significant research but contributes his own wise and thought-provoking comments and reflections on the after-life and the excellent information that has helped many become free from the toxic beliefs of cults and organized religion. It is a book which I highly recommend, not just on its merits for the excellent summary of the research, but for the broad range of condensed after-life investigations which offer a perfect springboard for further after-life exploratory material.

The research that Dr. Newton and Dr. Weiss' work and that of their highly-trained hypnotherapists worldwide have brought forth, curiously enough, is compatible with the information reported in the literally hundreds of thousands of reports of Near Death Experiences (NDE's). In his book, *Evidence of the Afterlife: The Science of Near-Death Experience*, Dr. Jeffrey Long summarized his 10-year study of NDE's. What is interesting is the correlation between the subject matter and the similarities that are being reported in all of these sources. Subsequently, Dr. Raymond Moody, and Dr. Jeffrey Long's investigations on NDE's, and the works of Dr. Weiss and Dr. Newton reveal a very similar pattern that appears delicately woven in the whole fabric of what we know today of the afterlife.

Another phenomenon that can't be ignored is that known as Pre-Death experiences (PDE). The work of John Lerma M.D. and his accounts of terminally ill patients in a hospice setting is unprecedented. He wrote two critical books: *Into the Light* and *Learning From the Light*. Dr. Lerma gave me the impression of being a very compassionate physician who cares deeply about his patients. I was most impressed by the consistent, loving attention he gave his dying patients. His thorough documentation of the transpersonal experiences his terminally ill patients in hospice reported, has brought to light a consistent report of loving help from transitioned relatives and other intensely loving spiritual beings to help in their transition to the Spirit world. These reports were reliably correlated even among his non-believing patients, the agnostics, and atheists.

Dr. Raymond Moody's latest book <u>Glimpses of Eternity: Sharing A Loved One's Passage From This Life to the Next</u>, presents meticulous documentation of SDE's or Shared Death Experiences which thoroughly document thousands of accounts of people who have shared profound spiritual experiences while witnessing the death of their loved ones. It is a must read by all people in general, health care workers, and especially those who may have a family member close to making their transition from this life.

It seemed, that as I put one book down and made copious notes of essential quotes and citations for my research, I inevitably came across more books and more subjects and related subjects. It was as if, I was in school and my invisible teacher would lovingly tap on my shoulder and whisper in my ear: "Here's another book that you must add to your reading list." This process went on for at least 3 solid years. I compiled pages and pages of essential citations from all different facets of the afterlife.

Another one of those predominant authors that stood out for me was a man by the name of Garnet Schulhauser, who related the most incredible transpersonal experiences that completely changed his life (and my own). He has written three books: *Dancing on a Stamp*, *Dancing Forever with Spirit*, and *Dance of Heavenly Bliss*, with a fourth book released lately, *Dance of Eternal Rapture*. In the first book, the information contained within that publication amazingly corresponds to the data being reported by the fifty thousand hypnotherapy subjects in Dr. Newton's database and Dr. Weiss' research, as well (with a few minor exceptions).

I wrote Mr. Schulhauser an e-mail telling him how much I appreciated the courage he had to write these accounts. He called it, *his coming out of the spiritual closet*. Later, I commented on how vital Dr. Newton's research was for me and the impact it had on my life. I also mentioned that his accounts matched, for the most part, the descriptions that Dr. Newton's patients had also reported. I asked Garnet in my e-mail whether he knew about Dr. Newton and had he read any of his books. From one day to the next, I received his e-mail thanking me for kind words of praise for his work adding, that he reported having heard of Dr. Newton but had not the opportunity to read any of his books! I was floored!

Here was a vivid account of his mystical experiences that basically described precisely what Dr. Newton's patients had described. Evidential? Some of you may say yes, some of you may say no — that it's just coincidental. Or to the diehard skeptics they would say that he lied to me. But I choose not to believe that. However, you look at it, to me, it was a resounding validation of how this information would transform my life and my outlook on this life and the ever after.

CHAPTER 22

RELIGIOUS BELIEF SYSTEMS

"We are not human beings having a spiritual experience.
We are spiritual beings having a human experience."
~ Pierre Teilhard de Chardin

"The important question regarding spirituality is
not which God you follow but are you true to your
soul? Are you living a spiritual life? Are you a kind
person here on earth, getting joy from your existence,
causing no harm, and doing good to others?"
~ Brian Weiss

Occasionally, I would drive by a church that would have announcements in large letters: *Come inside and find out about the Good News!* Or the church itself would be called the Church of The Good News. I would have a fleeting nudge of positivity to then have it come crashing down as I remembered all the fear-based teachings that these institutions are so noted for and those which I was exposed to as a child. I want to emphasize that not all churches accentuate the negative and quite a few churches genuinely do make every effort to follow the principles of Jesus's teachings. The centerpiece of these principles is: "Love one another." Or, "Treat others as you would like to be treated."

However, Christians appear to believe that if you are so-called *saved*, then you have nothing more to worry about. And the teachings of Jesus? "Oh well, those are just suggested ways of living." Really? First of all, I never ever understood the concept of being *saved* or *salvation*. From WHAT am I being saved? And I can tell you that this goes back to my days of the Baltimore Catechism that Sister Gunda-Gunda taught. I would often say to myself: "What is this woman talking about?" "Does she ever make any sense?"

Like author Garnet Schulhauser, who grew up in the Catholic Church, I was taught as well, that God was the ultimate authority. He presided from the deepest recesses of the universe.... somewhere (maybe he was an old man with a frothy grey beard who lived in some remote, antiseptic, corner of the universe smelling like pine oil?). He was undoubtedly presented as an anthropomorphic god. According to the Church, God created all humans, and he sent them to Earth to serve His purpose (whatever that was). God expected us to conform to his laws and to his rules, which were, (surprise! surprise!), revealed to us by his Church.

As Mr. Schulhauser wrote in his book <u>*Dancing Forever with Spirit*</u>: "*God demanded respectful worship and adoration from everyone. And after we died, we would appear before God to receive his judgment. If we had paid proper homage to him and had followed his rules, we would be allowed to enter Heaven. But if we had broken his rules without making amends, we would be punished in hell for eternity. God was like a king sitting on a gold throne dispensing rewards or punishments to the souls who had finished their lives on Earth. In the eyes of the Church, it would be outrageous blasphemy for humans to consider themselves to be a part of God."* (*Dancing Forever with Spirit*. Kindle version Loc. 2237-2241).

From the very first moment as a child, and especially in the seminary, I heard this endless litany of lies. I knew that it was not credible and I felt very uncomfortable with this doctrine. It never felt right. My heart told me it wasn't right because it didn't *feel* right. But I went along with it because I didn't want to appear as the rebel or the one to challenge the authority of *Holy Mother Church* because as we were all told if we didn't conform, we would rot in hell.

Mr. Schulhauser further writes: *"The Church's version of God bestowed him with several negative human attributes. He was vain because he demanded to be worshiped by humans in special ways, and vengeful if we didn't follow his rules. He gave humans free will to act on Earth even though it meant that many of his rules would be broken. God would be a loving and forgiving deity to those people who stayed on the straight and narrow, but cold and heartless to everyone else."* (*Dancing Forever with Spirit*. Kindle version Loc. 2241-2245).

Mr. Schulhauser summarized my views of the Church's version of God perfectly: *"I came to realize later in my life that the Christian God was really an anthropomorphic deity created to help them (the Church) control the masses through guilt and fear. They gave their God the attributes of a despot on Earth since that was something they could easily sell to their followers. Thus, like a king or queen on Earth, the Christian God expected his followers to pay homage to him and obey his commands, failing which he would become angry and vengeful. The early leaders of the Church knew that a God with these characteristics would serve them well in their quest to control their followers."* (*Dancing Forever with Spirit*. Kindle version Loc. 2250-2254).

Roberta Grimes is another significant researcher and author who has, for many years, delved into examining the afterlife data. Also, a former Roman Catholic, Roberta exposes the corruption of the church going back to the first centuries of its creation. She talks liberally about the deletions and additions to the New Testament and the claims that the church bases the justification of its existence. She speaks freely about the main addition to the New Testament and which, by some magical stroke of the pen, gives all the authority of the universe to the church. That passage is: *"And I tell you that you are Peter, and on this rock, I will build My church, and the gates of Hades will not prevail against it. I will give you the keys of the kingdom of heaven. Whatever you bind on earth will be bound in heaven, and whatever you loose on earth will be loosed in heaven."* (Mathew 16:18-19)

This passage clearly illustrates the reptilian brain at work to exert its power and control over the masses. This edict eventually, would pave the way for the establishment of an institution of corruption. The first clue that it was humanly penned comes from the mention of Hades. Hell, or Hades does <u>NOT</u> exist. Hell is a construct of the reptilian brain; therefore, it could not have come from a Jesus Who embodied pure unconditional love and compassion; The Jesus Who is the antithesis of all human fear and Whose love and compassion excludes the concept of punishment and fear. These are expressions of human vibratory resonance of the lowest category. Little did the early church founders realize that one day the gap between the Spiritual realm and the earthly realm would narrow and today's wealth of after-life research would finally expose the liars and their lies. One of my most favorite quotes comes Roberta's book *Liberating Jesus*: *"What may be Christianity's worst fruit of all is the self-righteous certainty so many Christians have about their salvation and the damnation of others."* (Kindle, Loc. 231). The Christians are so quick to judge others and place themselves on a solid platform of incorruptibility because in their minds they thankfully have been *saved*. So many of the pseudo-Christians blatantly ignore the greatest commandment of all: *"Therefore all things whatsoever ye would that men should do to you: do ye even so to them: for this is the law and the prophets."* (Mathew 7:12)

The afterlife research clearly dispels any existence of Hell or Hades or those who might run this dark place, i.e., demons, devils and the fictional big boy himself, satan. As a matter of fact, most of all the afterlife research that I have examined explicitly states that there is no religion in the afterlife. If there were to be a religion, it would be pure unconditional love. The record of all of our deeds and misdeeds comprise the platform from which we grow and learn, thus, serving to move us up the ladder of spiritual mastery, and not be condemned and cast into some invented pit of darkness and punishment. The above passage, like many in the Bible, overwhelms us with the stench of exquisite fear and damnation, a tradition so unlike the love that the Rabbi Master Jesus abounds with and urges us to exemplify.

To quote Dr. Michael Newton: "*The idea that satanic entities exist as outside forces to confuse and subvert people is a myth perpetuated by those who seek to control the minds of others for their own ends. Evil exists internally, initiated within the confines of the deranged human mind. Life can be cruel, but it is of our making here on this planet. The spirit world is much too ordered to allow for such muddled soul activity. Being possessed by another being would not only abrogate our life contract but destroy free will.*" (<u>Destiny of Souls: New Case Studies of Life Between Lives</u>, Pg. 1415-1420 Kindle edition).

I agree with Roberta Grimes that Jesus is clamoring to be free from the pseudo-Christians. Jesus needs to be let out of jail. Otherwise, the modern-day false Christians will become their own Jihadists and wreak havoc in the world. In reviewing the Opposite Strengths program, this thinking demonstrates absolute polarization of non-evidence based Theoretical Thinking. That, in itself, is a hazardous mental and emotional condition. It is equal in every respect to the abomination of the Inquisition, a tragedy of murder committed by the churchmen of that era all in the name of Jesus.

So now we come to the question of Reincarnation. What's all the fuss? Is it true? Is it false? Why doesn't the church teach it if it is true? There are many explanations to that question. One of these is that the early church, under the influence of the emperor Justinian, and principally his wife, Theodora, promoted the revocation of the teaching of reincarnation as taught by Jesus. Quoting author Garry J. McDonald: "*Ecumenical Councils over time determined what was to be considered religious doctrine and what wasn't. Many scholars believe that the Fifth Ecumenical Council (553 AD) deleted most verses addressing reincarnation from the Bible. But why? The reasons are simple. The church elders wanted the general populace to believe that it was only through the church and its elders could anyone communicate with God or ever hope to reach heaven. This kept all power within the church versus within the people themselves. And since the elders were men, these kept women at a subordinate level as well.*" (*Wisdom Magazine, Why Christianity Rejected Reincarnation*). That evidence is kept to this day in the Vatican's Secret Archives, where few selected researchers are admitted and, then, only by a methodical and strict vetting process.

The other reasons which were given by many scholars why the church didn't want the populace to know about reincarnation were merely this: *"You have one chance to get it right, one life and that's it. So, you better do as we say and be obedient to our commands and those of the church."* As mentioned before, free will is the most sacred of human conditions, and the afterlife research is very clear about this. If reincarnation did not exist, it would, as Dr. Newton say, *"abrogate our life contract and destroy free will. These factors form the foundation of reincarnation and cannot be compromised."* (*Destiny of Souls*, Kindle pg. 76). We learn by exercising our free will, and since we can't just learn personal and spiritual mastery in one lifetime (or in academic terms by going to just one class or one semester), we must complete the various courses of individual circumstances within the complicated interplay of relationships and dilemmas. *"The solution for all of us to improve is staying with the process of continuing evolution to become better than we are."* (Dr. Michael Newton, *Destiny of Souls: New Case Studies of Life Between Lives*. Kindle pg. 330.)

In all fairness, not all churches are pushing the hell and damnation envelope. There are many competent churches like I mentioned before. Many great human beings do so much for mankind by following the principles that Jesus taught. These followers of Jesus' teachings, (I refuse to call them Christians), continue to lead by their example of helping others and express more and more the unconditional love that Jesus, like other masters and mystics, was (and is), as a pure expression of Source.

Many of the mystics and saints of the Catholic Church were followers of the principles that Jesus taught, and they *practiced* them. I have met spiritual giants in the church, many of them I met in the seminary, and others in Junior and Senior High School. They have been outstanding role models for me. Saint Mother Theresa, Saint Francis of Assisi, Saint Therese of Lisieux, Saint Padre Pio and many other mystics demonstrated what we are learning from the afterlife research, principally, that love is unconditional and the core essence of Source or Spirit.

The notion of an all-loving deity, the image of the Source or the Tao (terms I prefer over the overused and underrated word "God") that emerges from all of the research paints a very different picture from the old, underrated concept of "God." The Source is the creator of everything in the Universe and is the sum total of all that exists. Source is pure unconditional love which is the binding force that holds All That Is together. Some church experts would call this Pantheism, but I prefer to see it as Panentheism which according to Google, "is the belief or doctrine that God is greater than the universe and includes and interpenetrates it."

We emanate from Source, and we are divine in nature and becoming more expressive of our own divine nature as we progress through our multiple episodes in our spiritual evolution. Our souls are sparks of the Divine. We are divine in nature and made in the exact image of our Creator. Our goal is to transform our self-destructive behaviors and feelings and become more highly developed expressions of the Divine Spark that we already are, which is pure unconditional love and compassion. These are forces of the Universe that are beyond our feeble mind's understanding or comprehension.

The research further shows that there is only oneness and unity in the Universe. Everything is interconnected and interrelated. In Physics, the tenets of the exclusion principle illustrate the interconnectedness of the Cosmos as do the many views of quantum mechanics and the evolution now into Quantum Consciousness.

The Tao, Source, or Spirit has no opposites and therefore is the one, single, unifying life force or energetic pattern of All That Is. The Source as an all-loving entity refrains from judgment or condemnation. The Source as pure unconditional love grants free will to all to give us an opportunity to grow and learn from our mistakes. Thus, the growth of our soul fosters the attainment of mastery over our negative feelings, emotions and subsequent ill-fated behaviors.

Fear is nonexistent within the heavenly realms. An all loving Deity does not employ terror, for it is a destructive emotion limited to the human expression and is deeply embedded within the density of Earth's vibrational pattern.

CHAPTER 23

AFTERLIFE RESEARCH: HOW IT CHANGED MY LIFE

"She had kept well behind the safety barrier her entire life, but now she was standing there at the edge of the precipice for the very first time, fumbling blindly with the realization that there were other ways to live, at how intense and rich life could be."
~ Katarina Bivald

Afterlife research is not a new field of study. It began in 1975 with the breakthrough publication of *Life After Life* by Dr. Raymond Moody in which he describes his interviews with approximately 150 individuals who had a near-death experience (NDE). In this publication, Harvey Irwin and Caroline Watt in their book *An Introduction to Parapsychology* summarize the major points that Dr. Moody introduced to the public in 1975. Dr. Moody's collection of cases identified a standard set of elements in NDE's:

+ An overwhelming feeling of peace and well-being, including freedom from pain.
+ The impression of being located outside one's physical body.
+ Floating or drifting through the darkness, sometimes described as a tunnel.
+ Becoming aware of golden light.
+ Encountering and perhaps communicating with a *being of light*.
+ Having a rapid succession of visual images of one's past.
+ Experiencing another world of much beauty. (page 159).

Dr. Helen Wambach in 1984 wrote her best-seller *Life Before Life* in which she describes the reports of her patients, who under hypnosis, relate past lives and their lives between lives. Dr. Wambach was a published precursor to Dr. Michael Newton's research. Her research consistently duplicates Dr. Newton's work which wasn't released until the early '90's.

Following Dr. Moody's and Dr. Wambach's research, Dr. Michael Newton's and Dr. Brian Weiss' research launched in earnest a wave of afterlife research that we are currently witnessing. Psychologists and Psychiatrists, especially those practicing hypnotherapy, dared to risk the reporting of the same results that Dr. Newton was writing about in his first book *Journey of Souls* in 1994, and his second best-seller: *Destiny of Souls* in 2001.

There is an impressive collection of afterlife research that is currently on the internet that overshadows any assembly of this type of research that I have ever seen. That work was assembled by Michelle Szabo and

Dr. Dennis Grega. It is awe-inspiring and a must for any researcher of the afterlife. In my opinion, it is the most extensive database of afterlife research description and analysis on the internet. Visit their website, and I assure you that you will be most impressed by its collection of information both modern and ancient.

One of the most impressive and evidential techniques concerning the mitigation of PTSD is the work of Dr. Alan Botkin, a Clinical Psychotherapist who at the time was working for the Veteran's Administration. He discovered a variation of EMDR (Eye Movement Desensitization and Reprocessing) in which veterans who had been subjected to trauma due to the death of fellow combat soldiers, or about victims of their own firepower suddenly brought them in contact with these deceased individuals in an altered state of consciousness. These visions were vivid and real to the patient and in which the victims or those who had transitioned would tell them that everything was OK. In other cases, the victims would offer their forgiveness in an ambiance of total and unconditional love. Dr. Botkin's technique is called IADC or Induced After Death Communication. His exact method is being replicated by hundreds of therapists whom he has trained through his organization, The Center for Grief and Traumatic Loss.

Included here are the summaries of the descriptions of the numerous accounts of NDE's (Near-death experiences) and PDE's (Pre-death experiences) and SDE's (Shared-death experiences). This information is compiled from thousands of all of the above references. Statistically speaking, the accounts come from believers and non-believers alike and from all cultures and national backgrounds.

I caution the reader to understand that these critical points which I have researched may seem very strange, especially when viewed outside the context of the original material. Thus, I encourage you to read one or more of these publications to appreciate the richness of the information presented. I encourage you to pace yourself and measure your intake of information. Sometimes, reading too many books on the subject can be overwhelming. Ask your Higher Self to guide you to the book that would be best for you with which to start out. Our Higher Self, our Higher Intelligence, Source, Spirit, or whatever you wish to call the All That Is, knows what is best for us at the time of our most pressing need. Source knows our needs best.

To summarize, here are some of the highlights that I have rescued from all these resources. It would be impossible to list all of the most essential citations that I have diligently categorized in my 4-year research study; however, I will list the ones that had particular significance for me and which literally collapsed the PTSD I had been experiencing over the years. Some of the points listed below are repetitive but worth re-emphasizing.

The multi-disciplinary and evidentiary research confirms the following:

+ Death is an illusion. We do not die; our physical bodies cease to function, but we continue to live in a more realistic and more conscious environment. We shed the body like a snake sheds its skin.
+ As reported by the majority of individuals (both believers and non-believers) involved with NDE's, PDE's, SDE, PLR and LBL experiences, the afterlife is one of infinite beauty, love, and peace which is beyond our imagination. It's a realm of ecstatic existence basking in the ever-present love of the Infinite.
+ The research is very clear about the non-existence of the devil, demons, hell, etc. These are mythological constructs invented by the church to exercise control over the masses through fear and trepidation. It seems that some humans are experts at using the reptilian brain to its advantage.
+ We experience our life on earth as one completing a course or courses in a semester in high school or college. We learn the lessons planned for that semester, and when we are ready, we move to the next step in our learning process. Does it not seem reasonable that to continue to learn we must move to the next classroom for the next lesson? We can learn to be masterful only with continued practice and application in varying circumstances. These lessons are more challenging to acquire in an ambiance of pure love and harmony that, according to the research, characterizes the afterlife. The same applies to our

spiritual evolution. We cannot learn all that we need to learn in one lifetime, so we come back to complete the lesson or work on a new one.

+ Most often than not, we come back with the same souls with whom we initially had to learn a particular lesson. Each soul in our soul group may take different roles and incarnate as different sexes in different lifetimes. Your uncle in this lifetime may be your sister in the next, your mother could be your brother, and so on and so forth.

+ The question that is most often asked regarding reincarnation is the following: "If we've had previous lives, why don't we remember them?" That is an excellent question, and the answer is simple. If we remembered all our past lives and all the negative things that we did or that were done to us, that would create such an emotional and mental crisis that we would not be able to function. It would incapacitate us from learning the lessons for this lifetime. If some traumas in this life cause us dangerous levels of anxiety or PTSD, imagine remembering the injuries of all of our lives! Another important reason for the amnesia is the fact that, if we recalled our past roles with the people we have incarnated in this lifetime, current challenges to overcome past transgressions would no longer be challenging. In other words, it would no longer be a challenge because it would be like the teacher giving out answers to the test questions before taking the test. Incoming amnesia guarantees a clean slate with the obstacles freshly presented to us in the hopes of obtaining growth thru learning and mastery. This includes dealing constructively with negative emotions, such as fear, anger, envy, etc. The quality of our relationships in any lifetime determines this rate of growth and learning, or the lack thereof.

+ The afterlife is made of Pure Unconditional Life. There is <u>NO judgment</u> in the afterlife and punishment is non-existent. We are, however, keenly aware of our errors and shortcomings and we are guided lovingly by our Higher Self or Divine Presence, and our Guides to examine what we could've done better. The idea or concept of sin or sinners is a judgment. That also is non-existent in the after-life. We are our own judges. But we are also taught in the life between lives to assume a position of compassion and forgiveness for ourselves and other souls with whom we incarnated in our previous life or lives. Transgressions are instruments of learning for our soul's growth and development.

+ Earth is one of the most challenging classrooms in the Universe. Souls who decide to incarnate on Earth are indeed brave souls. We, as souls choose to incarnate on Earth to achieve a more expedient mastery of our spiritual evolution. We can also arrange not to embody again. Our free will is always respected in the afterlife.

+ We all have Guides or highly evolved spiritual souls who have been with us for eons. They perform the roles of our directors and/or teachers in our many incarnations. They know us better than we know ourselves. They guide us and counsel us at inner spiritual levels, but they do not solve our problems for us. Again, that would be like the teacher of the class giving the answers to all the exams. The challenge is for us to confront our problems and pass the exams ourselves. But our Guides are always with us and never abandon us. When we ask them for help, they will provide the best assistance to help in the resolution of our challenges.

+ When our soul disembodies and leaves our earthly shell, we are met by our Guides and/or a *receiving committee* of relatives or other souls in our soul group. Sometimes, souls are met only by their Guides, and a Life Review is conducted with them before proceeding to meet with our Council of Elders or Council of Wise Ones.

+ The research further shows that upon completing a lifetime, the Life Review highlights all the good and the not so good behaviors we engaged in that lifetime. Furthermore, we feel how other people were affected by our actions, again, actually experiencing feeling the good or bad effects those behaviors had on others. For example, if you abused someone, let us say verbally, you will experience the exact same feelings that that person felt when you yelled and cursed them out. But again, no one judges us. We are our only judges. We examine what we could've done better and how that may have created a different outcome.

* Our Council of Elders is comprised of between 3 to 12 spiritually highly evolved Beings of infinite love and compassion. Going before these Beings is reported to be one of the most ecstatic and exhilarating spiritual experiences we as souls can experience. Most of the now 50,000 subjects who have undergone LBL sessions with the Michael Newton Institute trained hypnotherapists, report that being in Their Presence is as close as we get to the Eternal Source or the All That Is. The Council looks upon us with total compassion and love and praises us for all the excellent progress we have made no matter how small or large that may have been. They are instrumental in guiding us to explore the lessons we yet have to master, and they assist us in selecting the options or choices for future incarnations to further tackle our growth challenges. We come before the Council after completing each lifetime and once again before incarnating in the new life to come. We are reminded of our trials and are given the highest encouragement to be successful.

* We all have soul groups of 15 to 40 (or more) souls with whom we incarnate over and over again. We practice completing or perfecting our lessons together.

* We have life planning sessions before incarnating, and we have these sessions with the assistance of our Guides and are overseen by our Council of Elders or Council of Wise Ones.

* The Law of Karma is very much a part of how our next life will be set up. Karma, in simple terms, only means the balancing of energy or deficiencies of that energy in a previous lifetime. Karma is <u>NOT</u> punishment. For example, if I was a tyrant in an earlier lifetime, I may have to experience being the object of tyrannical behavior so that my soul will have the experience of feeling the effects of tyranny in my life. Thus, I will develop the awareness or the knowledge and wisdom to avoid that behavior in the future. Furthermore, Karma permits ample exploration of

the feelings of compassion, or the emotions of putting ourselves in other's shoes. This is so that we can understand others better and as well minimize the judging of others and ourselves.

There is so much more information that I have not been able to include in this brief summary of what has been for me a transforming experience. At this point, all I can say is that this information impacts me at the soul level. It resonates deep within my soul like no other information has in the past. In other words, it falls within the purview of an all-loving Source that resonates deep within the spark of the divinity within my being. My soul seems to cry out: *Finally, I see and feel the truth.* And then I remember the words of the Master: "*Ye shall know the truth, and the truth shall make you free.*" (John 8:32).

CHAPTER 24

PRINCIPLES OF FREEDOM FROM FEAR AND LIES

*"Fear, to a great extent, is born of
a story we tell ourselves..."*
~Cheryl Strayed

"When a thought hurts, that's the signal that it isn't true."
~ Byron Katie

I conclude with a synthesis of all the spiritual information that I have presented so far in the form of basic principles of my truth, that you may identify as truthful for you as well and adopt, some or all as your own. These principles did not come to me as a *download* from the Universe, but rather from the depths of my own spiritual reality. Although deeply personal, I share these with you my reader in the hope that you will find them useful to follow in your life. It matters not whether you are recovering from a nasty divorce, have lost a dearly beloved one, whether you are experiencing pain and suffering from wars or conflicts or the mental and emotional abuse of toxic belief systems. May these principles help you and guide you through your recovery process.

Principle One – Pure Unconditional Love

There is no proper name for "God." There is no proper description. Some refer to a genderless *Source, The Tao, Yahweh,* or *All That Is.* However, how can you name the unnamable and describe the indescribable? You can't. However, the word "God" has been so misused it could never even come close to describing the indescribable. As the Tao Te Ching says: *"The Tao that can be told is not the eternal Tao. The name that can be named is not the Eternal Name. The Unnamable is the Eternal Real. Naming is the origin of all particular things."* (Chapter 1. Translation by Stephen Mitchell). The Essence of Pure Divine Unconditional Love cannot be described or explained. It is beyond description or definition. I believe, though, that you can feel the Source as the Universal Truth of Pure Unconditional Love. The Unfathomable cannot be anything else because Love is the all-encompassing energy that holds all life within Its embrace as a Unified Whole. It is the glue that embraces all features of creation within its loving awareness. As Max Planck, one of the most prominent theoretical physicists of all times was quoted in 1944:

"All matter originates and exists only by virtue of a force......

We must assume behind this force the existence of a conscious and intelligent Mind. This Mind is the matrix of all matter."

Principle Two – If It is Reptilian- Dismiss it Immediately

The opposite of Pure Unconditional Love is fear, anxiety, self-denigration, guilt, hate, shame, self-loathing, violence or any other harmful feelings and consequent behaviors. Where there is love, there cannot be fear. This would also apply to belief systems (includes political belief systems) that promote those toxic feelings. Typically, fear-based poisonous belief systems are products of the reptilian brain or the primitive brain (the Limbic system that houses the amygdala) therefore they originate at lower vibrational frequencies of the human mind and *not at the higher Divine frequencies*. Besides being lies, these beliefs are the products of human ideas. The Opposite Strengths program identifies it as non-evidenced based Theoretical Thinking. They are akin to *stories* that we are told by others (or by ourselves).

Summarizing once again, the reptilian brain, housed in the Limbic System, or the emotional brain cannot think or reason. That function is left to the Prefrontal Cortex or the human part of our brain. The Limbic System acts to protect us from harm, real or imagined and is our survival mechanism. *Toxic beliefs are only factual within the cranial boundaries of the individual propagating or entertaining those beliefs. They are NOT REAL outside those cranial boundaries.* I heard a famous spiritual teacher recently say that phonetic sounds coming from the mouth of a person cannot represent the truth or that which IS. And I fully agree. Fear laced sounds are just that – sounds – or phonetic utterances that spew garbage out from the reptilian brain. You will encounter some life events, after reading this book, where your fear response will be triggered by any number of stimuli, be those stories or pictures, or what have you. When your fear is triggered, just remember you can dismiss it because it is of human origin and does not come from Source. You can dump it just like you dump your garbage. Apply B. Katie's process of Inquiry to discover the lies of fear that are exclusively human (Principle 6). Remember, Source is pure unconditional love.

Principle Three – Published Does Not Mean Necessarily Truthful

The Bible is reported by many to be the absolute word of God and taken literally by thousands. I do know that the Bible or Torah exposes many inspiring and deeply profound passages. But the Bible also has many contradictions. The Bible is laced with fear-based, reptilian thinking. I personally believe that many parts of the Bible were inspired by a Higher Power. But as I read individual segments, I also notice the human mind and its reptilian influences diligently at work. The books were written in times when fear and ignorance were the norms. It was a time when science was unknown and superstitious practices were the mainstay of the masses.

There is also much controversy surrounding the meanings of specific words that were translated from the original manuscripts. These mistranslations are the cause of high concern among many scholars because they completely changed the intended denotations. In some cases, it gave conflicting interpretations. Superstition and fear influenced the authors of the Bible. The Bible has been edited and re-edited over and over again by individuals, many within the context of their respective belief systems. They modified it to fit their paradigms (Paradigm Cramming) or concepts of what their god would say or do. Numerous inspiring and uplifting passages in the Bible cannot be ignored like: *Love thy neighbor as thyself* (the central theme of all world religions), or Corinthians 13 in the New Testament. I think it is incumbent upon the believer to listen to his or her heart as to what resonates as truth for him/herself.

> *"In the New Testament there is internal evidence that parts of it have proceeded from an extraordinary man; and that other parts are the fabric of very inferior minds. It is as easy to separate those parts, as to pick out diamonds from dunghills."*
> ~Thomas Jefferson. Letter to John Adams, January 24, 1814

Besides the Bible, we have millions of publications (including online social media outlets such as Facebook) that clamor for attention in salute to the truth that only represents the limited, if not outrageously false proposals and ideas of the deranged human mind. Again, *published* does not mean truthful (and that includes this book). Careful analysis and fact-finding are critical to determining the veracity of alleged facts. But listening to our heart's message of confirmation is the sure way to find comfort and solace. This can only be accomplished by quieting the mind in meditation.

Principle Four – Beliefs are Generational

Belief systems are handed down from generation to generation. Information is typically changed or adapted to the transmitter's leanings as it is passed down throughout the ages. Data is transformed, modified, and influenced by the transmitter's personal prejudices or social norms of the time. Many cultures in the world lack a written format to record their stories or beliefs and thus rely on oral traditions. Oral traditions are defined as: *The spoken relation and preservation, from one generation to the next, of a people's cultural history and ancestry, often by means of storytelling.* (The Free Dictionary).

Referring back to the Opposite Strengths Program, individuals who lead by Dependent, non-evidenced based Theoretical Thinking, generally don't question authority. They tend to just go along with whatever everyone else is doing or believing. And that is followed by *And if you don't have faith in this you're going to hell* or other such nonsense.

Principle Five – Numbers Don't Make Truths

Just because thousands, if not millions of people subscribe to a belief system, does not mean that the belief system is accurate. Like Giordano Bruno, a 16th-century Italian martyr, said: *"Truth does not change because it is, or is not, believed by a majority of the people."* He was burned at the stake by the maniacal Inquisition because he refused to call the Catholic Church inerrant or incapable of error.

Millions before the year 1492 believed that the earth was flat and if they ventured beyond the sight of the shore, they would fall off the planet or be eaten by sea monsters. Millions of people were proven wrong by Christopher Columbus' observations of physical phenomena (curvature of the earth and the rising mast of incoming ships) and his subsequent and successful trips to America and back to Europe. Just because it's fashionable to believe something does not make it accurate. Again, just because information is presented on TV, on the Internet, or is disseminated by books, the news media or lectures does not make it right either.

Principle Six – Thoughts and Feelings are Connected

We cannot have a feeling without it first being a thought in our mind. The exception would be in a fight/flight situation when the amygdala will prompt immediate action should you be in danger. For instance, if you are about to cross the street, and you turn and see a truck coming out of nowhere toward you at full speed, you most likely are going to get out of the way. The amygdala will bypass the frontal cortex (the thinking, rational part of our brain) and cause you to step back onto the sidewalk and out of harm's way. So, a thought, depending on its nature, is going to generate a feeling. The quality of the idea will determine the quality of the emotion(s) and the ensuing behaviors. B. Katie Byron's book: *Loving What Is: Four Questions That Can Change your Life* invites us to ask:

a.   "Is it true? (how do you know it's true?)

b.   Can you absolutely know that it's true? (what evidence do you have to believe that it is true?)

c.   How do you react when you believe that thought? (what kind of feelings and behaviors does that thought stimulate in you?)

d.   Who would you be without that thought?" (How would you be feeling and acting differently as a result of giving up that thought?)

e. Now, turn it around (reverse the statement you made up to reflect the total opposite experience or event)."

For example: "My husband doesn't love me anymore because I'm fat."

Turn Around: "I don't love my husband because he thinks I'm fat."

"I have never experienced a stressful feeling that wasn't caused by attaching it to an untrue thought. Behind every uncomfortable feeling, there's a thought that isn't true for us."

~ B. Katie

Principle Seven: Identify False Prophets by Their Fruits

"Beware of false prophets, who come to you in sheep's clothing, but inwardly they are ravenous wolves. You will know them by their fruits. Do men gather grapes from thornbushes or figs from thistles? Even so, every good tree bears good fruit, but a bad tree bears bad fruit. A good tree cannot bear bad fruit, nor can a bad tree bear good fruit. Every tree that does not bear good fruit is cut down and thrown into the fire. Therefore, by their fruits, you will know them." Matthew 7:15-20. Them refers to false prophets. In modern terms, they could also refer to any leader of an organization, church, political party, etc., who propagates any series of paradigms, meme's, beliefs, proposals and subsequent consequences of following or not those proposals. Fruits are again, the mental constructs that proceed to qualify, give status, or give an interpretation of events that happen around those constructs. For example, the late Fidel Castro may have said that all Cubans are to follow the Cuban revolution and the dogmas that validate the social reforms which those paradigms dictate. Some of the dictates are: *We will have a "democracy" by having elections, but only the communist party members can run for government posts.* And Mr. Castro would have probably have paraphrased: *I, Fidel Castro, will run for Prime Minister and then President but nobody can* oppose me.

Cuban citizens who don't follow these dictates and oppose the system, are incarcerated or worse, they are executed. So, there is a loss of free speech (an infringement on the sacredness of free will). The feelings that ensue are fear, anxiety, paranoia, or loss of freedom. These are reptilian feelings because they stimulate the Fight/Flight/Freeze Response and the behaviors that follow generally induce stress, depression, oppression, anxiety and other destructive attitudes and actions. Political as well as religious leaders can be very cunning in how they present information. At first glance, it may appear to be innocuous, but upon closer examination the information presented is a downright lie or falsehood. When these seemingly innocent teachings eventually produce fruits that rot the mind and the soul to its core, is when we realize we have been deceived. The weavings of deceit permeate these arguments and are typical of any tyrannical and authoritarian regime. I have observed that tyrants accuse others of precisely what they are guilty of doing.

Principle Eight – Everything is Inter-Related and Interconnected

Science, and in particular the strange marriage of physics and modern spiritual thinking, is demonstrating that there is an intrinsic unity to everything in the Universe. All things are interrelated, interconnected and everything is part of the Whole. There is only <u>ONE</u> power, <u>ONE</u> Presence, <u>ONE</u> reality. That reality is beyond our understanding and comprehension. Western paradigms are geared toward duality (God vs. the "devil") as opposed to the Taoist (Oriental) mind that concentrates on unity thinking and oneness through the complementary opposites of Yin and Yang, masculine and feminine, night and day, etc. All opposites complement each other within a unified field of all possibilities. No force or presence opposes or goes against the ONE. It is impossible! And the Source manifests Itself through all of its expressions. Those expressions are you, me, and every living being in this Universe.

Principle Nine – Duality is a Myth

The Eternal Source has NO opposites. There is no duality in this sense of the word as there are no satans, devils, demons, or evil forces. People act out of their own free will and are not influenced or forced to behave by these fictional ideas or concepts. The research previously documented bears testimony to this truth. But more importantly, my conscience tells me that it can't be right because it does not fit the reality of an all-loving, all-powerful Creator.

The terrorists who propagate these vile and inhumane ideas are only misguided, polarized human beings who want to exert their power and control over others by instilling in them fear and terror. This Neanderthal thinking is based on fear and superstition. I would like to think that the human race has gone beyond these old sets of beliefs. Yes, the Earth really is round!

Unfortunately, there are those who are polarized and suffer from paradigm paralysis. There is no going forward for these individuals until they see beyond their hateful, self-serving beliefs. Free will is sacred. It is given to us by Spirit to allow us free range to make choices. And the choices we make will have consequences that eventually we will endure, as a learning experience in our spiritual progression, whether these choices caused harm or good to others or to our environment.

Those who propagate reptilian beliefs are responsible for the terror and fear that they instill in others. Karmic law dictates that they will have an opportunity to grow and to learn from their actions so that they can become more aware of how fear affected others. This may reveal itself through fearful situations themselves, or some other consequence that would best help the soul grow and learn.

The beliefs propagated by certain individuals that an evil opposite is out to get you to commit evil or "sinful" acts are absurdly false. This includes the notion that certain *entities* attach to you to cause you to commit wrongful acts or engage in uncharacteristic behaviors. I call this <u>The Geraldine</u>

Effect which is mirroring Flip Wilson's famous female character's line: "*The devil made me do it.*"

In my continuing research about the after-life, I have found there is a wealth of information that has come forth, especially within the last 5 to 10 years, that is very profound and important. My approach has been multi-faceted, and I aim to paint a broad-brush stroke of all the aspects in the field. Just recently, I was reading a book from a fairly prominent author and YouTube mogul. The book was on consciousness and the range of vibratory patterns of people, places, things, etc. Initially, I was impressed with the author's knowledge of quantum physics, string theory, etc. I also applauded the author's emphasis on positive belief systems as opposed to fear-based ones. I thought to myself, *so far so good, I like what I'm reading.* Then out the blue, the author described how homeless people who walk in the streets babbling to themselves are vibrating at a very low frequency and to quote the author: "Have entities attached to them that babble through them." I took a double take and couldn't believe what I was reading. This author went from the heights of quantum physics and positivity to the depths of pre-historic, superstitious jibber-jabber, all in one fell swoop! This statement was a *cut and paste* line that I heard come out of the TG's mouth so many times. I instantly detected the cultist influence and promptly returned the book for a refund.

My question is this: How can a seemingly intelligent individual who appears to be well read and has done his homework in quantum physics suddenly descend to those levels of insanity? The answer is not forthcoming for me, and it appears that the power of cultism is so persistently pernicious that it is the downfall of many a well-intentioned individual. As Dr. Newton so eloquently has stated, we live in an orderly spiritual world where this muddled activity is not the norm. The Geraldine Effect means that we can blame an outside *force* for our behaviors. Thus we are no longer responsible for those behaviors. If this were true and paraphrasing Dr. Newton, free will would be abrogated, and reincarnation would have no purpose. That is not how Spirit works.

In my opinion, this misguided belief, and the individuals who spread these lies can cause detrimental harm to individuals, especially those who are already unstable, physically, mentally and emotionally. Assuming that this ridiculous statement was true, i.e., *attached entities cause homeless people to babble*, could the author have stated it differently? Perhaps something like: "Mentally ill individuals tend to vibrate at lower levels of frequencies due to their unstable brainwave patterns?" or something similar to that? Why instigate needlessly fear as a platform for discussion? That narrative needs to be re-examined by those who profess to *know* instead of politely speculating possibilities. My point is if you're going to risk making a speculative statement, do so positively keeping in mind the welfare of others.

As educators, as reporters of the research, or as humans caring for other humans, do we not bear a deep and profound responsibility to those we teach, inform, or educate, either verbally or in a written format, not to harm them with fear and dread? I address all individuals, whether they be speakers, teachers or authors, and especially in spiritual or religious fields. Be conscious that among your audiences there will be those who have been gravely wounded by the gloom and doom of fear-based beliefs. So, we need to be very careful, not only what we say, but HOW we mean it. We bear a profound responsibility to help these individuals avoid furthering their mental and emotional anguish. And I need to remind my colleagues that there are hundreds of thousands, if not millions of us who have gone through the hell of fear-based lies and deceptions and are still very fragile of mind and spirit.

Duality exists, in a sense, that humans express fear, anger, desperation, vindictiveness, judgment, etc., versus pure unconditional love which Source embodies and which we desire to express more completely. These dualities arise in the expression of our individuality to help us learn from them. Thus, paving the way for us to communicate purer unconditional love in our lives. Source desires to experience love through us and gently lead us back to His/Her loving embrace.

The Judeo-Christian tradition, and all of the major religions of the world, apparently lay out the edict: "Love thy neighbor as thyself." Loving your neighbor means that you don't scare them with lies and evil threats! These people who preach hell and damnation, are giving you a clear mandate to find the nearest exit and use it before it's too late! The fear mongers want to have power and control over your mind and more importantly, your pocketbooks. They are the wolves in sheep's clothing. This includes those individuals who make you engage in behaviors, (*in the name of God*) that you feel and know are wrong. If the results of a concept or practice make you feel sad, shameful, anxious, fearful, or any other destructive feeling or emotion, abandon it immediately. Then, should it become necessary, find professional help to get you through the emotional ordeal. This book may help you in many ways that you did not previously imagine. Trust the process!

Principle Ten – Your Inner Wisdom is Your Best Teacher

There are no Gurus, teachers, or any authorities (that includes me!). There are wise and evolved souls in this world who can point to many paths, but they are not THE path! We need to listen to our core more. Our heart is the spokesperson for the soul. Our heart vs. our mind is the one to ultimately give us the green or red light on any decision we need to make for our best good and well-being.

To quote Krishnamurti:

"The primary cause of disorder in ourselves is the seeking of reality promised by another; we mechanically follow somebody who will assure us a comfortable spiritual life. It is a most extraordinary thing that although most of us are opposed to political tyranny and dictatorship, we inwardly accept the authority, the tyranny, of another to twist our minds and our way of life. (J. Krishnamurti, *Freedom From the Known*, pg. 11)

Is it a wonder that we were absolutely prohibited from reading Krishnamurti? During the process of my recovery, I remembered that

Krishnamurti was on the banned list and that prompted me to want to read him even more. Why was I told I couldn't expose myself to his works? There must be something the deranged cultists didn't want me to know. And I am so glad I did!

Ironically, I was working in the early 90's for an international governmental training organization working with teachers from Central America. Our training was on effective school leadership and substance abuse prevention. On one occasion, we had our training, at a fundamentalist Christian retreat center in the mountains of northern New Mexico. Our group eventually decided to leave the center because the staff of the center complained that our participants were "too loud and the men touched the women too much!" We really scratched our heads at that one! It was here, amongst the ultra-conservative right wingers that I continued to read Krishnamurti and the above passage stood out in blazing words! When I read it, it felt like the doors of heaven had opened up to me! No wonder they didn't want me to read it! Ironically, it was also at that retreat center that I ran across the next quote from Krishnamurti:

"Truth has no path, and that is the beauty of truth, it is living. A dead thing has a path to it because it is static, but when you see that truth is something living, moving, which has no resting place, which is in no temple, mosque, or church, which no religion, no teacher, no philosopher, nobody can lead you to. To be free from all authority of your own and that of another is to die to everything of yesterday so that your mind is always fresh, always young, innocent, full of vigor and passion." (J. Krishnamurti, <u>Freedom from the Known</u>, pgs. 19-20).

I exercised my free will and flexed to the gift of my Risking Strength and ventured out to be embraced by the Universal flow of Divine Love and enfolded by the healing force of the Divine Healer. Either way, this journey has been a transformational experience for me, as it may have been for many of you. I hope that you will consult the bibliography and continue your studies. But remember the golden rules:

1. You do not have to believe anything that anybody says (or writes), especially if the information provokes uneasiness, fear, and anxiety. Respect where you are right now in your evolution.

2. If it is fear-based, it is of the reptilian brain. Therefore human, therefore invalid, and should be rejected. <u>Spirit does not present anything in fear – only unconditional love.</u>

3. Forgive yourself and then forgive others. This raises our vibrational field into a higher realm of love and helps us express the Source within us. We must have compassion for ourselves first if we can efficiently have compassion for our fellow mankind. And last but certainly not least:

4. Love others as you love yourself. Do unto others as you would like others to do unto you. Practice compassion and mindfulness. The more we love, the more love will elevate our vibrational field to new heights of Spiritual awareness. I want to conclude this writing with a quote by Bob Moawad:

"The best day of your life is the one on which you decide your life is your own. No apologies or excuses. No one to lean on, rely on, or blame. The gift is yours – it is an amazing journey – and you alone are responsible for the quality of it. This is the day your life really begins."

May the Source or the All That Is grant you peace and healing and many blessings now and in the future.

With love for the Source within and about you,

Patrick J. McKallick

OPEN LETTER TO CLERICS, BROADCASTERS, SPIRITUAL LEADERS, TEACHERS, AND COUNSELORS OF ALL FAITHS

I address this letter to all those who are responsible for the guidance and direction of those human beings who are seeking spiritual solace and comfort. You have all been given a grave responsibility to discharge your duties in the highest of standards according to your individual faiths. One of those responsibilities is the care for the overall well-being of your students, audiences, and congregants. One of those responsibilities is to convey messages of inspiration and love, free from all vestiges of fear, gloom and doom.

Do you remember when you were a little boy or girl and you sat in your place of worship and listened to your cleric, and you felt frightened by what he or she had to say? Can you recall the actual feeling you experienced when those words were uttered? Do you remember how you kept thinking over and over again the frightening words of doom that might befall you or humanity based on what that priest or cleric said? Did you experience nightmares? Did you worry endlessly about it?

What do you think happens today when you say almost word by word the same accounts of horror and fear and how that is affecting not only the small ones in your congregations, broadcasts, schools but also the older ones, especially the highly sensitive and unstable among your audiences? Do you genuinely think that is the right thing to do? But you may protest saying, "but in the Bible or the Koran or this book or that book," it says this and that and horrible things that are supposedly professed as being correct. But, do you genuinely think that the All That Is, the Source of all Being, Who is infinite Pure Unconditional Love would have authored such fear tainted discourses? Do you genuinely believe that? I think not! Only humans can propagate fear because their brains are conditioned and, in many instances, guided by that lower vibratory emotion.

Please take heed! Speak the language of the Higher Self and speak only the words of love and comfort and hope and positivity.

Remember the massive responsibility that you bear! You want to be able to look at your life when you pass on and say that you did the very best to instill positivity and fearlessness to all whom you touched. No one will judge you once you pass on to the next phase of your existence. Only you will decide yourself of your right or wrongdoing. The Great Eternal Source does not judge nor condemn, but brings loving attention to our growth and development in our journey Homeward.

Peace and Love,
Patrick J. McKallick

ADDENDUM

ALTERNATIVE HEALING PRACTICES

EMOTIONAL FREEDOM TECHNIQUE
OR THOUGHT FIELD THERAPY

In 2000, I was exposed to a significant mile marker. It was a technique that at first, I was very skeptical about. I had heard so many of my colleagues and fellow counselors talk about *tapping* and how it helped themselves and their clients deal with their fears and phobias without drugs quickly and efficiently. They were using this with their clients to help them reduce or lower the emotional charge associated with phobias, anxiety, panic attacks. As I was reviewing the information, it looked too good to be true. I thought to myself: *"here we go again, another new age BS technique."* But since I had had some experience with acupuncture, I thought there might be some merit to the process. So, I reviewed some VHS training tapes that a friend of mine had lent me. I was impressed with not only the results that the process was having on deeply distressed clients like war veterans but also how simple the process was. I applied the technique to myself and the issues I was dealing with at the time, and the results were truly amazing. It has been a real life-saver for me. I highly recommend that you investigate this further. You may consult the following website: www.emofree.com or just Google Emotional Freedom Technique.

MEDITATION

"Meditating is also a means for you to move beyond your analytical mind so that you can access your subconscious mind. That's crucial since the subconscious is where all your bad habits and behaviors that you want to change reside."
~ Joe Dispenza

One of the most important breakthroughs for me was cultivating the art of meditation. It helped me to get centered, calm my mind, and develop an ability to observe the thoughts that get me in trouble. Meditation is for me transcendence or the ability to rise above to a higher state of awareness and peace. Today, it is challenging for me to go one day without meditating for at least 30 minutes or longer. The day is just not the same without it. By quieting the mind, I am able to achieve the peace that is hard to explain. But also by calming the mind, I am open to a higher level of inspiration and consciousness that is healing and restorative.

Meditation takes practice. But, like anything else, the more you practice it, the better you get at it. The research on the health benefits of meditation is overwhelming. Meditation is indeed an evidenced based practice. Health professionals such as Dr. Deepak Chopra, Dr. Jon Kabat-Zinn and many scientists and researchers have proven over and over the benefits of meditation, including the art of Mindfulness. Jon Kabat-Zinn developed a Mindfulness-based Stress Reduction Program at the University of Massachusetts. Mindfulness is also an attribute of consciousness long believed to promote well-being. Sizeable population-based research studies have indicated that the idea of mindfulness is strongly correlated with well-being and perceived health. Studies have also shown that rumination and worry, contribute to mental illnesses such as depression and anxiety. Mindfulness-based interventions are useful in the reduction of both rumination and worry.

Meditation, as Dr. Deepak Chopra says is "going into the gap between one thought and another." The challenge is to prolong your stay in the gap as long as possible. According to Dr. Chopra, the gap is the *unified field of all possibilities*. It is the emptiness that creates all things. In the Tao-Te-Ching, Lao-Tzu in Chapter 10 says: "*Can you coax your mind from its wandering and keep to its original oneness?*" (Translation by Stephen Mitchell). Jon Kabat-Zinn compares the mind and all of its thoughts to the surface of the ocean in a storm. He likens each wave to a new idea, perhaps tumultuous in nature. He says though stormy above, once you go below the surface, there is only silence and peace. That is how he compares meditation, to an empty silence. The Taoists also equate emptiness to usefulness. That which makes a house useful is not just the walls and the roof but more importantly the void within the walls in which you live. Without the gap, you would have nowhere to abide.

A SPECIAL HEALING MEDITATION

I would like to share with you one of my most potent healing meditations. One morning, I awoke filled with worry over some health concerns. When I'm in any altered states like this, my immediate recourse is to sit down, close my eyes, and be silent. Once I've silenced my mind sufficiently, I go through the following guided imagery in my mind.

I take as many deep breaths as necessary to relax every part of my body from my toes to my head. Once I'm sufficiently relaxed and receptive, I imagine my favorite place in the whole world where I feel I can really feel calm and worry-free. For me, that is a beautiful tropical beach flanked by swaying palm trees and the melodic rhythm of the soothing ocean waves. If a tropical beach doesn't appeal to you, then perhaps you can put your attention on a mountain meadow or a lush park with thousands of flowers, or anywhere else you find peaceful and relaxing.

One morning, I asked my Higher Power or Divine Presence to send me a healing Being of Light. You can be more specific and ask for Jesus, Buddha, Krishna, Mohammed or any other Master. In my case, I let my creative consciousness take over from there, and I honored and trusted whatever imagery came through without any attachment to any specific outcome. I waited a short while as the representation came into my conscious awareness. Then, with a surprising glace, I saw that Jesus was walking by my side. I <u>felt</u> His Presence, and I <u>sensed</u> His Luminescent Being next to me. He took my hand and asked me what troubled me. I answered him not with words, but with my thoughts. I vividly felt us walking together splashing our feet in the warm, shallow waters of the last vestiges of the incoming waves. Our feet sank into the sand, and it gently massaged them to a relaxing caress. Then I allowed my inner creativity to put together the next scenes. I saw Jesus let go of my hand and turn to me and say to me in my thoughts, "Kneel before me so that I may place my hands on your head." I did so and felt a rush of indescribable love course through me from the top of my head to the bottom of my feet. I heard Him in my mind say *"May you be freed from the past and may you find peace in healing."* I got up, and he had vanished, and I emerged from the healing meditation feeling exhilarated with a profound sense of wellbeing and peace.

As I concluded my meditation, my fears had disappeared entirely, and I had a very peaceful day, a very, very different day. Curiously, shortly afterward as I was showering, a thought of doubt about what had just happened entered my mind. Immediately, I heard in my mind, *"Why do you still doubt?"* It was as clear as if somebody had whispered to me above the noise of the splashing water gushing out of the shower head. I hushed my doubts and gave thanks for such a profoundly healing experience. The next day, I came out of the Doctor's office with a clean bill of health. All that worrying for was for naught. Suffering comes, in large part, from too much thinking. And I might add, not just overthinking, but by believing that those thoughts represent reality.

I was surprised that my Higher Power selected Jesus to walk by me. In the last 30 years, I had developed such an aversion to Jesus. I suppose this was true for me because the Jesus I had been exposed to represented hate, discrimination, condemnation, and judgment. It was the Jesus of the Christian Fundamentalists, which I knew deep in my core was not the real Jesus. The Jesus in my meditation was so unlike that brand of Jesus. This was not the fake Jesus the Pseudo-Christians so ardently promote. He was a different Jesus. He was the loving, caring, enduring Being of Light and compassion from Whom Pure Unconditional Love and acceptance emanated in flowing abundance. If you still have an aversion to that old, worn-out version of the human Jesus, turn inward in meditation and meditate on the Real Jesus, He will make Himself known to you and not let you down.

ENERGY PSYCHOLOGY OR ENERGY WORK

There has been an emergence recently of various forms of healing modalities known as "Energy Work." Others refer to it as Energy Psychology. These formats have used Quantum Physics, String Theory, Quantum Entanglement, etc., to explain the basis for their effectiveness. There are many different healing modalities, from Reiki to Quantum

Touch to Reconnective Healing. There are comprehensive Energy Healing websites that you may want to consult on the Internet.

What I found over the years is that profound healing can come from healers who are not as mainstream. One of those healers is Christine Hart, M.D. She calls herself an energy worker, however, as she no longer practices allopathic medicine in the traditional sense, but relies on her knowledge of the human body which effectively compliments her energy work. I fortuitously was introduced to Christine through a mutual friend in Boulder, Colorado who highly recommended her talents as a healer.

Dr. Hart practiced family medicine for 35 years leaving her practice of traditional medicine to work exclusively as an energy worker. She has been working in the energy healing field now for about 15 years. Christine worked with the Lakota tribe and studied the Peruvian energy methods with Dr. Alberto Villoldo's Four Winds Society. She has experienced healing processes with the Shipido peoples of the Peruvian Amazon, as well. She teaches the Munay-Ki, a class offering the energetic rites handed down by the Q'ero shamans of Peru. The Munay-Ki class was another transformative experience for me as it seemed to finely tune my intuitive abilities.

In the past two years, I have had, approximately seven to eight healing sessions with Christine. These produced tangible and evidential results of profound emotional healing and reparation, primarily related to past people, places, things, and events. The sessions healed the scars of past traumas and brought a resolution of emotional conflicts which I, apparently, had unconsciously clung to at deep inner levels of my psyche.

Without saying, I highly recommend Christine's work. Besides being a highly competent healer, she is a kind, sensitive, and gentle soul. If you don't fall in love with her knowledge and know-how, you definitely will fall in love with her beautiful persona. In my opinion, she is a healer of the highest order and who does not let ego interfere in her wondrous craft.

Dr. Hart is writing a book about her experiences soon to be published. In the meantime, she can be contacted through her website which is: www.energyprocesses.com (the process is plural: _processes_).

Patrick J. McKallick is a Cognitive Behavioral Counselor, Certified Neurofeedback Provider and international consultant and trainer. Mr. McKallick worked as a clinician, both nationally and internationally, in the administration of EEG Neurotherapy treatment for patients with alcohol and other drug addictions, ADD, PTSD, and other anxiety disorders. He conducted extensive training events regarding Neurofeedback for psychologists, psychiatrists, and other licensed counselors in the U.S. and in countries of Latin America and Europe. Earlier in his career, he was a lead trainer for one of the U.S. Department of Education's regional training centers. He worked extensively as a consultant in the areas of alcohol and drug abuse, organizational development and community mobilization for planned social change, principally for the U.S. Department of State, the Organization of American States, and the U.S. Agency for International Development, and numerous NGO's. He also has worked in the criminal justice system with high-risk offenders on probation. Mr. McKallick was born and raised in a rural area of north-central Mexico. He grew up in a bilingual and bicultural family. His early family life was unstable, violent, and traumatic. His alcoholic father abandoned him in an orphanage while his mother fled to the U.S deserting her husband's uncontrolled violence. Subsequently, he left to attend high school, and college in the United States, where he obtained a degree in Psychology and Sociology. As an author, he has written several professional articles for international journals and other scholastic publications on community mobilization and substance abuse prevention. He is also the author of professional articles and training manuals on Community Mobilization for Planned Social Change and technical manuals for EEG Neurofeedback, mainly in Spanish. Mr. McKallick continues to expand his knowledge of evidential after-life research. He is currently engaged in other writing projects on the subject.

BIBLIOGRAPHY

Brodie, Richard, *Virus of the Mind: The New Science of the Meme*. Hay House, 2009.

Capra, Fritjof, *The Tao of Physics*. Shambala, Boston. 1991

Capra, Fritjof, *Uncommon Wisdom: Conversation with Remarkable People*. Bantam Edition, 1989.

Chopra, Deepak and Tanzi, Rudolph, *Super Brain: Unleashing The Explosive Power of Your Mind to Maximize Health, Happiness, and Spiritual Well-Being.* Harmony Books, 2012.

Craig, Gary. *The EFT Manual: Emotional Freedom Techniques*. Energy Psychology Press, 2011. www.EFTuniverse.com.

Desai, Panache, *Discovering Your Soul Signature, A 33-day Path to Purpose, Passion & Joy*. Random House, 2014.

Dreher, Diane, *The Tao of Inner Peace*. Copyright Diane Dreher, 2000

Dyer, Wayne Ph.D., *A New Way of Thinking, A New Way of Being: Experiencing the Tao Te Ching*. Hay House, 2009.

Dyer, Wayne Ph.D., *The Power of Intention: Learning to Co-create Your World Your Way.*, Hay House, 2004.

Gallo, Fred P. Ph.D., _Energy Tapping for Trauma, Rapid Relief from Post-Traumatic Stress Using Energy Psychology_. New Harbinger Publications. 2007.

Gallo, P. Fred, Ph.D., and Vincenzi, Harry, Ed.D. _Energy Tapping, 2nd Edition_. New Harbinger Publications. 2008.

Gordon, Richard, _Quantum-Touch, The Power to Heal_

Gordon, Richard, _Quantum Touch, Core Transformation, A New Way to Heal and Alter Reality_,

Gordon, Richard, _Supercharging Quantum Touch, Advanced Techniques_

Gordon, Richard, _Quantum Touch 2.0 The New Human: Discovering and Becoming_.

Katie, Byron, _Loving What Is: Four Questions That Can Change your Life_. Harmony Books, 2002.

Krishnamurti, J., _Freedom from the Known_. Harper San Francisco, 1969.

Lipton, Bruce H., _The Biology of Belief: Unleashing the Power of Consciousness, Matter & Miracles._ Hay House, Inc. 2008.

McTaggart, Lynne, _The Field, The Quest for the Secret Force of the Universe_. HarperCollins Publishers, Inc. 2007.

McTaggart, Lynne, _The Power of Eight: Harnessing the Miraculous Energies of a Small Group to Heal Others, Your Life, and the World_. Simon & Schuster, Inc., 2017.

Mills, Roger, Ph.D., _Realizing Mental Health_. Sulburger & Graham Publishing, 1995.Mitchell, Stephen, _The Tao Te Ching_. Harper Collins, 1988.

Newberg, Andrew M.D., Waldman, Mark Robert. _Why We Believe What We Believe: Uncovering Our Biological Need for Meaning, Spirituality, and Truth_. Free Press, 2004.

Thich Nhat Hanh, _The Miracle of Mindfulness: A Manual on Meditation_. Beacon Press, 1987.

Thomas, Thomas, Ph.D., Thomas, J.W., Ed.D., _The Power of Opposite Strengths: Making Relationships Work_. Opposite Strengths, Inc. 2011.

Watts, Alan. _TAO, The Watercourse Way. With the collaboration of Al Chung-Liang Huang_. Pantheon Books, New York, 1975.

Wolinsky, Stephen Ph.D., _Quantum Consciousness: The Guide to Experiencing Quantum Psychology_, Copyright Stephen Wolinsky, 1993.

Wolinsky, Stephen Ph.D., _The Beginner's Guide to Quantum Psychology_. Copyright Stephen Wolinsky, 2000.

Wolinsky, Stephen Ph.D., _The Tao of Chaos: Essence and the Enneagram_. Bramble Books, 1994.

Zukav, Gary. _The Dancing Wu Li Masters: An Overview of the New Physics_. Harper Collins, 1979.

TRANSPERSONAL SPIRITUALITY & AFTERLIFE RESEARCH BIBLIOGRAPHY

Alexander, Eben, M.D., _Proof of Heaven: A Neurosurgeon's Journey into the Afterlife_. Simon & Schuster, 2012.

Alexander, Eben, M.D., _The Map of Heaven, How Science and Ordinary People Are Proving the Afterlife_. Simon and Schuster. 2014.

Alexander, Eben, M.D. and Newell, Karen. _Living in a Mindful Universe: A Neurosurgeon's Journey Into the Heart of Consciousness._ Rodale Books, 2017.

Anthony, Mark, _Evidence of Eternity_. Llewellyn Publications, 2015.

Botkin, Alan, L. PsyD. _Induced After Death Communication: A Miraculous Therapy for Grief and Loss_. Hampton Roads Publishing, 2005.

Champlain, Sandra, _We Don't Die, A Skeptics Discovery of Life After Death_. Morgan James Publishing, 2013

Giesemann, Suzanne, _Messages of Hope. The Metaphysical Memoir of a Most Unexpected Medium_. One Mind Books. 2011.

Giesemann, Suzanne, _The Priest and the Medium_. Hay House, 2009.

Giesemann, Suzanne, _Wolf's Message_. Suzanne Giesemann, 2014.

Grimes, Roberta, *Liberating Jesus*. Christine F. Anderson Publishing & Media, 2015.

Grimes, Roberta, *The Fun of Dying*. Christine F. Anderson Publishing & Media, 2015.

Kagan, Annie. *The Afterlife of Billy Fingers*. Hampton Road Publishing. 2013.

Kelley, Mira, *Beyond Past Lives*, Hay House, 2014.

Kribe, Pamela. *The Jeshua Channelings, Christ Consciousness in a New Era.* Booklocker Books, 2008.

Lerma, John, M.D., *Into The Light*. New Page Books, 2007.

Lerma, John, M.D., *Learning From The Light*, Career Press, 2009.

Long, Jeffrey, M.D., with Paul Perry. *God and the Afterlife, The Groundbreaking New Evidence of Near-Death Experience*. Harper Collins, 2016.

Martini, Richard., *It's a Wonderful Afterlife: Further Adventures in the Flipside., Volume One*. Homina Publishing, 2014.

Martini, Richard., *It's a Wonderful Afterlife Volume Two: Further Adventures in the Flipside (It's a Wonderful Afterlife Book Two)*. Humana Publishing, 2014.

Martini, Richard., *Hacking the Afterlife: Practical Advice from the Flipside*. Homina Publishing, 2016.

McKenna, Bill., *The Only Lesson*. Balboa Press, 2011.

Moody, Raymond, Jr. MD, Ph.D. with Paul Perry., *Glimpses of Eternity. Sharing a Loved One's Passage From This Life To The Next*. Guideposts, 2010.

Moorjani, Anita, *Dying To Be Me: My Journey from Cancer to Near Death to True Healing.* Hay House, 2012.

Morgan, Mikey as told to Carol Morgan with Roberta Grimes, *Flying High in Spirit: A young Snowboarder's Account of His Ride Through Heaven.* Christine Anderson Publishing & Media. 2015.

Newton, Michael, *Journey of Souls: Case Studies of Life Between Lives.* Llewellyn Publications, 1994.

Newton, Michael, *Destiny of Souls: New Case Studies of Life Between Lives.* Llewellyn Publications, 2001.

Newton, Michael, *Memories of the Afterlife: Life Between Lives Stories of Personal Transformation.* Llewellyn Publications, 2009.

Newton, Michael, *Life Between Lives: Hypnotherapy for Spiritual Regression.* Llewellyn Publications, 2004.

Pitstick, Mark, MA, DC., *Soul Proof: Compelling Evidence You Are an Infinite Spiritual/Energetic Being.* 2006.

Rynes, Nancy, *Awakenings from The Light.* CreateSpace and Amazon. com; Solace Press. 2015.

Schulhauser, Garnet, *Dancing on a Stamp.* Ozark Publishing, Inc. 2012.

Schulhauser, Garnet, *Dancing Forever with Spirit, Astonishing Insights from Heaven.* Ozark Publishing, Inc. 2015.

Schulhauser, Garnet, *Dance of Heavenly Bliss, Divine Inspiration for Humanity.* Ozark Publishing, Inc. 2015.

Schulhauser, Garnet, *Dance of Eternal Rapture.* Ozark Publishing, Inc., 2017.

Schwartz, Robert, *Your Soul's Gift: The Healing Power of the Life You Planned Before You Were Born*. Whispering Winds Press, 2012.

Schwartz, Robert, *Your Soul's Plan: Discovering the Real Meaning of the Life You Planned Before You Were Born*. Frog Books, 2009.

Smith, Peter, *Quantum Consciousness: Expanding Your Personal Universe,* Consciousness Collective Publishing, October Grey Media., 2015

Tucker, Jim, M.D., *Life Before Life: A Scientific Investigation of Children's Memories of Previous Lives.* St. Martin's Press, 2005.

Tucker, Jim, M.D., *Return to Life: Extraordinary Cases of Children Who Remember Past Lives*. St. Martin's Press, 2013.

Weiss, Brian, MD., *Same Soul, Many Bodies: Discover the Healing Power of Future Lives through Progression Therapy*. Free Press, 2004.

Weiss, Brian, M.D., *Through Time Into Healing: Discovering the Power of Regression Therapy to Erase Trauma and Transform Mind, Body, and Relationships*. Simon and Schuster, 1992.

Weiss, Brian, M.D., *Messages from the Masters: Tapping into the Power of Love*. Grand Central Publishing, 2000.

Weiss, Brian, M.D. and Amy E. Weiss, M.S.W., *Miracles Happen The Transformational Healing Power of Past-Life Memories*.